AWESOME CHRISTIAN EXPERIENCES

Awesome Christian Experiences

▼

A collection of true stories showing God at work in the lives of people

Buddy Holbrook

Writers Club Press

San Jose New York Lincoln Shanghai

AWESOME CHRISTIAN EXPERIENCES
A COLLECTION OF TRUE STORIES SHOWING
GOD AT WORK IN THE LIVES OF PEOPLE

iUniverse books may be ordered through booksellers or by contacting:

Writers Club Press
an imprint of iUniverse.com, Inc.

iUniverse
1663 Liberty Drive
Bloomington, IN 47403
www.iuniverse.com
1-800-Authors (1-800-288-4677)

ISBN: 978-0-5951-5348-0 (sc)

Print information available on the last page.

iUniverse rev. date: 01/08/2020

Excerpt From "Resurrection"

Tim reached out his right hand, took the dead man's right hand and spoke loudly and authoritatively, "In the name of Jesus Christ, I command you to get up."

With that he pulled.

What happened next? Read "Resurrection"

Excerpt from "Dewberry Number Two"

"Do you see this chicken leg? Far back in eternity, long before man or the Earth were created, God predestined that I, on this date, in this place, at this table, should eat this piece of chicken."

Smiling triumphantly, his point well made, he began to raise it toward his mouth.

To find out what happened read "Dewberry Number Two"

Also By Buddy Holbrook

The Legend Lives On
A collection of short stories

No Justice In This County
A collection of short stories

CONTENTS

To Begin.......................

Just to get this all started, the stories you are about to read are varied. Some of them are a little funny, some are a little weird, some you may consider inspirational and others are just here. React as you please. All the stories have one thing that binds them together. They're all true. Sometimes, you may think I'm stretching that, but it's a fact. Until you see a disclaimer otherwise, no matter how far out, you are reading real history, history which is in some fashion part of my life. I've been a wanderer, been a lot of places, seen many people and held a variety of jobs. These are some things which happened to me and things which happened in places where I was.

Let me explain that word 'awesome' in the title. This isn't a book of just hoop-te-do, hallelujah, miracle stories, although those are certainly included. 'Awesome' means attention-getting, something that makes you stop and think, something that may just make you smile or something that reaches way down deep inside you and holds on for days. It was originally derived from the word 'awe'. Some of these stories are the sort that hold us in awe.

I am by profession a talker, having been a preacher, teacher, missionary and evangelist. I have been a few times a writer and have had my own radio show. Most of these stories are told here in story telling fashion, that is, as though I might be relating what happened to you orally, like in a sermon, a broadcast, in an informal discussion or even a bull session. A few are done in writing style. You'll know the difference. Read on. Enjoy. Oh yes, thanks for spending your money buying my book. God bless you as you read.

STORY ONE
WHEN WOMEN PRAY

▼

God does indeed work in strange ways to bring about the answers to our prayers. Often what Christians pray for, especially the women, concerns moral problems in the community. I ran across a couple of incidents that tie together on that theme.

The first, was in the town of Taft, California. I was a pastor there for seven years. Taft began as a camp for oil drillers back in 1910. There were tents and a saloon on a hilltop overlooking the valley below where the drilling was going on. When they finally struck oil, they hit a gusher so big that oil flowed across the valley floor like a river. People came with mule-pulled wagons filled with barrels that they filled by dipping buckets into the oil.

That caused the opening of the Sunset-Midway oilfield and the camp on the hill got even bigger. Then some houses began to be built. A little town began to spread down the slopes of the hill. The settlers decided to call it 'Moron.' They said you had to be a moron to live there. The name stuck. When the town got big enough to apply for a post office, the Post Office Department refused to set up an office in a town called Moron. The people decided to name the town Taft in honor of the man who was then president of the country.

About halfway down the hill, a dirt street developed that was only one block long. In that block were five houses of prostitution, all in a row on the north side of the street. The big problem facing those business people was the fact that while the town had been growing, a bunch of churchgoing, moralistic types had moved in, including a bunch of wives. These good Christian ladies, and some of their husbands, began to pray, quite seriously, about getting rid of the prostitutes.

For months they prayed. Finally, one night, a very strong wind blew in from over the hill on the west side of town. Some said it was the strongest wind they'd ever seen. At the height of the storm, for some reason unknown to this day, the house of prostitution on the west end caught fire. The girls and their customers got out just in time. Before anyone could do anything about that house, the fire spread to the next one. Driven by the strong wind, it leapfrogged from house to house till all were burning brightly. Before anyone could begin any attempt to stop the blazes, all five houses were just piles of ashes on the ground.

Maybe the owners took it all as a sign from God. The ladies who worked there left town. The houses were never rebuilt. Fact is, history doesn't record that there ever was another such house in the town.

For another look at unique answers to prayer, we go all the way from Central California to eastern Ohio. The town is the farming community of Garrettsville. I was there in 1975 for a week of ministry with the local Baptist church. One rather dark, cold night I was riding with the pastor and his wife, Ron and Pat Peoples, to a home out in the country. We came to an intersection of two farm roads. Visible there were a few remains of what had been a building. I asked about it.

Pat told the story like this. That building had been a bar, one with a rather notorious reputation. Every week at their morning prayer meeting, the ladies prayed for God to remove that menace from their community. Late one night it happened. The bar burned. Being out in the country, away from the town, it had no fire protection. It burned to the ground. Apparently there was no insurance. Most of the damage was cleaned up but the building wasn't rebuilt.

The next week, the ladies gathered for their morning prayer meeting. They were all excited about how that major prayer had been answered. As the talk was going on, the maid who worked for the lady in whose home they were meeting was heard to say, "Humph, you ladies pray and talk. I put some feet on my prayers."

Did the maid burn the bar down? They never got another word from her, but all the ladies are convinced that in this instance God got some help.

STORY TWO
RESURRECTION

▼

Jump forward in time. We're back in the town of Taft, California, but it is now the early 1980's. Up on the hill where the town began as a group of tents, it's all now houses and a Baptist church. At that time, I was pastor of that church. Right where the saloon had been years before, my office now sat.

When the town had really took off growing, they had gotten rid of the tents and built a school on the site. Later on the church bought the site, tore down the old school building and put in a new building. When I became pastor, we expanded the building, taking into the building the area where the bar had been. In the education wing of the church we also had a seminary extension center.

We met every Tuesday night for three hours, seven till ten. Several of the students were oilfield workers. One was a young man named Randy Bright; an excellent student. One Tuesday night, Randy came in all excited. He told the following story. He was an eyewitness. Knowing that it was rather incredible, I wrote down the names of the participants. I've kept that piece of paper all these years. Several times, I have told the story. Here it is, believe it or not. Oh yes, I am changing the names of the chief players, except Randy.

Randy was a member of a five-man maintenance crew for one of the major oil companies. They spent their working days riding around in a big truck going from well to well doing whatever routine maintenance was necessary. There was a two-way radio in the truck for communication back to the office they worked out of.

There were in the crew two men who were rather ardent Christian witnesses, Randy and one other, a fellow we'll call Tim Lakes. They were continually sharing with the other men the blessings they were receiving from God. Most of the fellows took it in stride, OK with them. There was one man, we'll call him Harvey Sanders, who was a rather ardent unbeliever. Randy and Tim made it a point to always be witnessing directly to Harvey. He made it a point to be totally antagonistic to Christianity and to loudly reject anything they attempted to tell him. He wanted nothing to do with 'getting saved 'because it would interfere with my lifestyle.'

On this particular Tuesday, during lunch Randy had been witnessing to Harvey again, with the same negative results. Just after lunch, the driver pulled the truck up to what they call a location. That's a place where there is an oilwell. What they had to do there only required one man to go over to the wellhead and read a meter. The foreman told Harvey to go. The rest of the crew sat in the truck watching.

When Harvey got near the pump on the well, he suddenly fell over like someone who'd fainted or had a heart attack. It was instant. One second he was walking along as normal as usual. The next, he's on the ground. One man started to get up.

"Hold it," said the foreman, "Don't anybody go out there."

The foreman, a man with years of experience in the field, knew that there was only one thing that could cause that reaction, hydrogen sulfide gas. This gas, known as H2S, is colorless and odorless. On rare occasions, a pocket of it will be hit underground or it will seep into a well shaft. Then it seeps out into there air. When you come into contact with it, you don't even know you've done it. When you breathe it, the effect is instant, death within seconds.

Someone asked, "Why don't we do something?"

"Too late," the foreman said.

"Get on the radio and call an ambulance," said another.

"Too late. He's dead."

They sat and looked, amazed.

"Somebody's got to do something."

Tim volunteered. "I'll hold my breath. I can do that long enough to drag him away from the well into clean air."

"OK," said the foreman, "Just don't breathe."

Tim ran out to the well, grabbed Harvey by the hand and drug him back to the side of the truck. They checked. No pulse; no breath. He was dead.

"What can we do?" one man asked.

Tim reached out his right hand, took the dead man's right hand and spoke loudly and authoritatively, "In the name of Jesus Christ, I command you to get up."

With that he pulled. Harvey came to his feet and stood on his own. The man who had just been declared dead stood among them alive.

His first words were a complete surprise to everyone, "I've got to get saved right now. Somebody pray with me!"

Randy and Tim immediately volunteered. The 'dead man' got on his knees, unashamedly right there by the truck in front of all the crew and asked Jesus to come into his life and be his savior.

Was Randy excited that night at class? Everyone was!

*   *   *

Short Take. On a Sunday morning, I passed two ladies standing in the center aisle who were reading the announcements in the day's church bulletin. As I passed one said to the other, "Somebody needs to tell the secretary that 'association' is not abbreviated 'a s s'."

STORY THREE
STEVE

▼

While we're talking about dead people and weird happenings, let me tell you about my old friend Steve. When my wife, Becky, was a student at Grand Canyon College, one day she brought him home. He was in one of her classes. That's when I met Steve. We became instant friends. Later on we became ministry partners, working together in southern Arizona and in Mexico. He was a great singer, a fine preacher and a fantastic personal witness. His one other talent was personal counseling.

We also became business partners. I became the pastor of a new church in Lake Havasu City, Arizona—home of the London Bridge. Steve dropped out of college and went along as my music leader. Since it was a new church, neither of us got paid, so we went into our own construction business contracting mostly with local real estate agents. It was fun.

I left Arizona to go to Texas for further seminary training. At the same time, Steve left and went to Minnesota. That's where his old Air Force buddy George lived. He got a job in a factory that made pacemakers and spaceship parts for NASA, a company called Mimco. He also carried on an extensive ministry, usually being in different churches four times every Sunday. As was his custom, he also witnessed to everyone on his job. He was well-known and liked.

After a couple of years, he moved back to Phoenix and once again enrolled in college. While in Minnesota, he had met a girl and fallen in love. After he moved, they kept up a long distance romance which ended in marriage a year later. A few years later, his old friend George moved back to Phoenix. It was a joyous reunion.

Steve moved his new wife into a small place several miles west of Phoenix out Highway 60. He went to work for the state of Arizona. That gave him a rather long commute into town and back each day.

I had made a couple of moves and didn't see him for several years. Then, my old friend Bill died and I was asked to return to Phoenix to do his funeral. I saw Steve there. It was a real pleasure to see him again. He told me all about his job, how he was doing a lot of personal counseling and witnessing. He was really enjoying it.

He told me about the many young adults who worked where he did, about their personal needs, their problems, their bad habits and how he tried to maintain a good witness to them. He let them know, in a non-pushy fashion, that he cared, and that he believed there was a solution to many of their problems in a personal relationship to Jesus. Having known and worked with Steve for so long, I had no doubt that he had a very effective witness which was doing those people a lot of good. One of the people Steve witnessed to in the office was a young single mother we'll call Linda. She had a little girl. We'll see more of her later.

Steve also told me about how he and his wife were in the process of attempting to adopt a baby. It seems he was incapable of fathering a child. As it worked out, three weeks after I saw Steve, he and his wife became the parents of not one but two adopted babies at the same time. What a life change!

One week after the babies came to their house, Steve was killed in a traffic accident. It happened like this. He was driving home in the afternoon along a stretch of the highway that was out in the countryside between two small towns. No one knows for sure what happened. It is known that he had spent a lot of the previous nights staying up late with the babies. Possibly, he dozed off. There is also the fact that he had to drive home facing the setting sun. Just possibly the sun blinded him. Maybe it was a combination of factors.

All anyone knows for sure is that Steve's car crossed the centerline and ran head-on into a motorhome. He was killed instantly. Here is where it begins to get strange. It had now been eleven years since he had left the job in Minnesota. There was a secretary who had worked on the same job who had known him well but had had no contact with him in the intervening years.

On the day Steve had hit the motorhome, this secretary, we'll call her Anne, was driving home from work in Minneapolis. She patiently faced the afternoon bumper to bumper traffic. Suddenly, she wasn't on that crowded street anymore. She was driving on a strange highway, which seemed to be far out of any city. Then it happened. In the road in front of her car stood Steve. It was strange how she recognized him instantly after all those years. Before Anne could hit her brakes, he started to rise up in the sky. In absolute defiance of all natural law, he just rose up and out of sight.

Then, Anne was back on the street in Minneapolis facing the commuter traffic. There was one startling difference. She was now two blocks from where she last remembered being and had no idea how she had gone that distance. Puzzled beyond comprehension, she drove on home.

Steve died on Thursday. Due to the fact that many people had to come a long way for the funeral, the service was delayed till Tuesday afternoon. Many of the people at the office where he worked planned to take the afternoon off to attend. Linda, the single mother, was one of them. Although she had refused Steve's entreaty to become a Christian, she was profoundly influenced by him and respected him very much.

On Monday night, Linda put her little girl to bed and soon afterward put herself to bed in the other bedroom. She lay facing the outside bedroom wall in the dark. The light came on. Linda knew it had to be her child wanting something. As she rolled over to speak to her daughter, it registered in her mind that the overhead light was not on. There in the corner of the room was a fantastically bright light. In the center of the light stood Steve. Linda knew she wasn't asleep or dreaming. She was awake. This was real.

Steve began to speak, "Linda, you must accept my God. You must become a Christian. You really must."

There was an extreme urgency in his voice and an air of confidence as he continued, "Find George. He'll help you. Tell my wife I love her and the kids."

He was gone. The room was dark. She did not know anyone named George. Steve had never mentioned that name to her before. How would she find him? Maybe he'd be at the funeral.

Here I was the day of the funeral, just thirty days after I had been to Phoenix to bury my dear friend Bill. Now, I was back at the same funeral home for another service. Again, it was packed to capacity. At the service, everyone was given a printed program. It listed three speakers. The second was a man named George. It was obvious to Linda that this had to be the man. Following the service a long procession went all the way across town and out north to the cemetery. Linda followed along.

I was riding with my friend Neal, the same man I had ridden with to Bill's burial. We went back to the same cemetery. Weather conditions were exactly the same as a month before. Talk about deja vu!

When the interment service was ended, most of the people began to leave rather quickly. It was a long way back to town and time for commuter traffic to begin. Linda stayed behind. George noticed her. He figured she was from Steve's office and went over to talk to her. He introduced himself. She looked happy to see him.

"George," she said rather anxiously, "I've got to talk to you."

"Well, follow Shelly and me home. We'll talk there."

At George's house, Linda told him about Steve's appearance. Together with Shelly, they talked and prayed. Linda became a Christian that night. The last I heard, she was in regular contact with George and Shelly.

George had called his dad, Gus, in Minneapolis on Friday to tell him about Steve's death. On Tuesday evening Gus remembered Anne, the secretary from Steve's job. He thought she might be interested in knowing about his death. He dialed her number on the phone. While it rang, he reminisced about how long it had been since he had last talked to her. She answered.

"Hello Anne. This is Gus."

"Gus, am I glad to hear from you. You won't believe what happened to me the other day."

She related the puzzling incident that she had experienced going home on Thursday.

"Anne, Steve got killed that day, that time, on the road you described."

At about the same time Gus was talking to Anne on the phone, back in Phoenix Linda was praying with George and Shelly, making Jesus the lord of her life.

Thinking back about Steve, the years we were together in business and ministry and the time we just spent being friends, three things come to mind. The first is the last time we talked. As I said previously, it was at Bill's funeral. Steve was his usual, full-of-life self. He jumped from subject to subject telling me all about the things that were going on in his life.

There was one incident that particularly amazed him. It had happened just the week before. He was totally animated as he related it to me.

He taught a Bible study class every Sunday morning. One of the ladies who attended regularly was in the hospital. As was his habit, he was concerned about her and packed a hospital visit into his already overcrowded schedule.

At the hospital, he sat in her room talking. She had a tumor, as she said 'the size of a grapefruit.' She was, naturally, fearful of the surgery. She wanted Steve to pray for her. She trusted him as a spiritual leader and believed in his prayers as a spiritual power.

But, there was more. She had read in the Bible a passage about how sick people should ask the elders of the church to anoint them with oil and pray for healing. She believed that if Steve would pray for her, she would get well.

Here, Steve was a doubter. He'd never had anyone make such a request before and he didn't know if it would work. Divine healing was out of his area of expertise. But, because she sincerely wanted him to try, and overlooking his own lack of faith, he prayed asking God to heal her. Soon after he left, filled with doubt.

The next morning when the hospital personnel came to prep the lady for surgery, she was definitely different. They called in the doctors. X-rays were made. The tumor was gone. It had completely disappeared. The doctors were puzzled. They ran tests. They had no choice but to pronounce her cured.

She went home. From there she called Steve. He was as puzzled as the doctors, but he rejoiced with her. When he told me about it, he was still amazed and overjoyed. And, he was looking forward to trying it again.

The other two incidents I want to tell you about are things we experienced together. The first happened in a coffee shop one night. We'd worked all day and stopped in for refreshment and a business discussion. When we were ready to leave, we walked up to the register to pay the bill. The cashier was a young lady neither of us had seen before.

Steve spoke to her, "It's going to be allright."

"What?" she said in total surprise.

"It's going to be all right, those personal problems you've got."

"How did you know I've got problems?"

"Well, I guess God told me. It's your problems with your kids and your ex-husband." He went into a few details.

"Everything you're saying is correct."

"You are to quit worrying about it right now. Everything is going to be OK. No more problems."

"You're really sure?"

"I'm sure."

She looked relieved and happy. As we left the restaurant I questioned him about it.

"Oh it happens all the time," he said.

It's no wonder the man's death was unusual. It simply followed the pattern set by his life.

Finally, there's the cat story. We had been over to Neal Borst's house one night and were headed back to my apartment. Just before reaching a stop sign, the car in front of us ran over a cat, killing it.

We stopped. From the bed of Steve's pickup we got a shovel and a scrap of plywood. It would be a shame to leave the cat's body in the street. We picked it up on the plywood, laid it in the back of the truck and went home.

At the back of the parking lot was a cottonwood bush. We buried the cat under it. As we packed the last shovelful of dirt over the grave, I began to fill philosophical.

"Steve, there was some life there. Maybe not a soul as we understand it, but there was life that animated the body. Now it's gone and the body is dead. Where did the life go?"

"Oh, back to the source of all life, I reckon."

At his interment, as I stood beside the casket saying the last words over his body before the burial, I told that story. It just seemed appropriate. I felt like Steve had returned to the source of all life.

My last words were these, "It may not be good theology, but it works for me."

STORY FOUR
LET THERE BE LIFE

▼

The year was 1918. The whole world had been engulfed in the Great Influenza Epidemic. Millions around the globe were dead and more were dying every day.

In the USA, in the state of Georgia, just north of the town of Atlanta, a few miles out Peachtree Road in the country was the settlement of Doraville. One of the residences in Doraville that faced Peachtree Road was a small house that had begun its existence as a log cabin. It belonged to Fred Holbrook and his wife Willie. The original one room had been expanded as the years went by to accommodate their growing family.

In the bedroom that was just off the front room of the house, Fred and Willie's oldest son, Ree, age sixteen, was in serious physical jeopardy. There appeared to be a distinct possibility that he would not live to be seventeen. It wasn't the flu that was putting him at death's door. It was pneumonia-double pneumonia. Like the flu, there was no known cure for pneumonia, not even a good treatment, although people kept trying different things and hoping for the best.

One morning Willie went into Ree's room to check on him. He'd gone into a coma. She got no response from him. His breathing was slow and labored. Fear struck deep into her heart. She sent word to the doctor to please come to see Ree as soon as was possible. The doctor was a busy man in those days of much sickness, few cures and the custom of doctors making house calls. It was late in the evening when he reached the Holbrook house on Peachtree Road.

The doctor went into the room where Ree lay in his bed. The young man's fever was high. The bedclothes were wet with his sweat. The doctor knew that both lungs were infected to the point of losing their ability to function. The end had to be near. Willie and Fred watched as the doctor examined this son who was the pride of their life, the fruit of their love. The sadness on the doctor's face spoke volumes.

"Come on, folks," the doctor said, "let's go into the other room."

In the front room, with the door to the bedroom still cracked open, the doctor spoke, "Fred, Willie, Ree's at the end. He's far beyond anything anyone can do for him. He'll be dead by morning. I'm sorry."

The doctor went out into the cold darkness of the winter night leaving Ree's parents in the front room to grieve for the son who was not yet dead. Willie shut the door to his room. She and Fred sat watching the fire burn.

What no one knew was the fact that in the coma, Ree was aware of everything going on around him. He knew the doctor was there. He heard what the doc told his parents. He was just weak, sick, under the domination of the illness. He would have felt better if he wasn't aware. Or would he?

In the darkness, he gathered up his strength. First, he overcame the struggle and got his eyes open. There was nothing to see but the little light coming through the crack under the door. There was no sound coming from the other room. Apparently his parents, weakened by their efforts, had dropped off to sleep. Ree was alone.

He struggled, pulled himself to a position of forcing his body off the bed, his knees on the floor, and his elbows on the damp covers. In the darkness, he spoke to the one hope available to him.

"God, only you can help me. I'm sick. I'm not ready to die. I want to live. Mostly, I want to live to serve you. Please make me well. Thank you. Amen."

He forced his way back into the bed, under the covers and went to sleep. Whether he lived or died, his mind was at ease.

During the night, Willie and Fred went to their bed. Early the next morning, Willie rose from bed and walked into the kitchen. There sat Ree at the table, happy, smiling, dressed and well.

"Hi, Mom, what's for breakfast?"

Three years later, Ree got married. Shortly after that he became the pastor of the Bethel Baptist Church. He was still serving God as a pastor when he died at age sixty-six, fifty years after his predicted death.

Not long before Ree died, he sat with me one day and told me this story. He'd gained his life by faith and for the next fifty years he lived his life by faith. By the way, Ree was my dad. I'm his youngest son.

Story Five
Tell Your Friends

▼

Randall was a long haul trucker. Along the way, he'd picked up a few bad habits, like heavy drinking. Whenever he was in town between loads, he spent a lot of time in local saloons, making friends and taking care of his habit.

One day Randall got sick and spent a long time in the hospital. While he was there a preacher visited and witnessed to him about Jesus. Randall decided that's just what he needed. He accepted Jesus as lord right there in the hospital.

This was such a life changing experience that Randall decided as soon as he got well and got home he had to witness to all his friends. He got home and called everyone he knew to meet at his house on Saturday afternoon. He didn't tell anyone what the purpose of the meeting was. They'd find out when they got there.

On Saturday, he had the living room all set up with all the chairs of every variety he could find around the house. At three o'clock, the appointed time, the chairs were all full of excited, expectant people who were talking happily to each other, wondering what the meeting was about. There was much speculation about a drinking party

Randall got up before the group and made an announcement, "Friends. I want to tell you all about the fact that while I was in the hospital, I accepted Jesus as my Savior. I'm a born again believer."

Immediately every man in the room got up and walked out the door. There Randall stood, just him and Jesus.

STORY SIX
THE RAPTURE

▼

In a previous story, I mentioned Steve and his friend George. They were in the Air Force together, stationed at Luke Field near Phoenix. While they were there Steve became a Christian. Very soon after that, he began telling George that he also needed to make the same decision. George resisted. That was not for him.

Steve really liked George, but he was ardent in his Christianity. He knew what a change it had made almost overnight in his life. What he wanted was for his good buddy to have the same joy. So, he tried different approaches. None worked. Then, at church, Steve learned about the second coming of Jesus. He also learned that in connection with that there was to be an event known as The Rapture.

For any readers who are not familiar with that idea, the Bible teaches that near the end of time, Jesus will come with his angels into the atmosphere of the Earth and call out all those who are believers. They will immediately disappear from the planet, all of them, everywhere. It is further believed that after that event, things on Earth will get extremely bad, in every possible way. Hell will be manifested right here for all who get left behind.

Steve thought that telling George about The Rapture and all the bad that would go on afterward would be an incentive for him to become a believer. Nope, that didn't work either. Steve tried. George resisted.

One nice afternoon, George was going west out Camelback Avenue, driving out to see Steve. It's a four lane street. As George approached a red light driving in the curb lane, he noticed that the car already stopped in the center lane had a Christian symbol on the back. He pulled alongside it and stopped, looking over at the man who was driving.

Then, he looked up at the light, then back at the other driver. He was gone! George's first thought was 'The Rapture has come. It's come; he's gone; I'm left!'

Suddenly George was very frightened. About that time the other driver reappeared. He had bent over to pick something up from the passenger side of the floor. George was relieved. Then he thought, 'What if it had been true?'

Imagine Steve's surprise when, five minutes later, George was knocking on his door anxiously saying, "Come on, Steve, you've got to tell me now how to become a Christian."

God does indeed work in mysterious ways.

*   *   *

One of the ladies of the church had been continuously bothering the young pastor, propositioning him about sex.

Finally, one day he could take it no more. "I'm going to tell you what night you can sleep with me," he said. She perked up, "Oh good, when?" "The last night I'm on Earth," he said, "You come down and get in my casket and sleep all you want to." At last, he had killed the subject. Never heard it from her again.

STORY SEVEN
MEET MY FRIEND

▼

It began at the Olivet Baptist Chapel in Phoenix. I was serving as interim pastor while the sponsoring church decided the future of that mission. Jim Winger had been sent out by the home church to be the music director.

There was an elderly lady, Mrs. Pruitt, who was present at every service-Sunday morning, Sunday night and Wednesday night. She always came alone. One Sunday, we got a little better acquainted and I asked about her personal life.

"Are you married?"

"Yes, I am, but my husband isn't a Christian."

"That would explain why you come to church alone."

"Yes. He has no interest."

"Do you think he'd mind if Jim and I came by for a visit?"

"No. He's not antagonistic, just not interested. But, you're welcome to come."

"How about tomorrow night about seven?"

"Fine. Let me give you directions."

They lived out in the country west of town on a farm facing one of the main roads that ran through that side of the valley. Jim and I arrived a few minutes after seven. The driveway led to the back door. The outside lights were on as though we were expected.

As we drove up three huge dogs came running from near the house and began barking in dead earnest. We sat in the car. In a minute, Mr. Pruitt came to the back door and called them off. They quietly sat down. We got out and went in.

Both Pruitts greeted us warmly. She gave us both a cup of coffee as we passed through the kitchen. We all then went into the living room and found chairs.

The conversation began lightly on a 'let's get acquainted' basis. We learned a little basic history about the Pruitts, how long they'd been out there and the fact that they were now retired, actually in their seventies.

I decided to turn the conversation a bit more serious.

"Mr. Pruitt, I want you to know how glad we are to have your wife as part of the church and tell you that you are welcome anytime you feel you'd like to attend."

"Thank you, Preacher, I've never been too much of a churchgoer. Running the farm kind of kept me busy seven days a week."

"I understand."

I then steered the talk around to his personal beliefs, which he shared with me on a friendly basis. Just as I reached the point of asking him about his relationship to Jesus, he suddenly had a complete change in the look on his face. He looked at me in complete anger. It was like a new person had swiftly entered the body of the old man. He began to speak loudly, his voice and visage filled with wrath.

"What are you two people doing coming out here bothering me? Who asked you to come out here anyway? Why are you in my house talking all this stupid talk I'm not interested in?"

"Excuse me, sir. If you've got a problem with us being here, we'll go."

I glanced over sideways at Jim and Mrs. Pruitt. Both were as surprised as I was at the change. Jim had a look on his face like he was afraid we were about to get shot or some such. He had his eye on the door we came in.

"That's right," the old man shouted, "I want you to go. I want you out of my house. Leave. Leave now!"

As Jim and I headed toward the kitchen and the back door, Mrs. Pruitt looked as though she wanted to say something. I nodded my head and raised my hand to indicate it wasn't necessary. Mr. Pruitt followed us to the door as though to make sure we'd get gone and do it rapidly.

I was worried about those dogs much more than about the man. When we exited, the dogs didn't move. Apparently coming from the house, we were OK. We got into the car. Mr. Pruitt was standing by the back door with that defiant look still on his face. I cranked up and backed out.

Jim's comment was, "Wow. Can you believe that?"

I stopped at the end of the driveway and spoke to Jim.

"Jim, the day will come, and soon, that he will want us and be glad to see us. There will be a change and soon. Count on it."

Two Sundays later, Mrs. Pruitt had a worried look on her face in church. After the service, I asked her about it.

"It's my husband. He's in the hospital. It's really serious. He nearly died Friday night. I don't know if you'd be interested to visit him or not or even if he'd want you to."

"I'll go by tomorrow at afternoon visiting time."

"Thank you."

On Monday afternoon, I was at the hospital and got admitted to the ICU. There lay Mr. Pruitt with the usual paraphenalia of tubes and IV bottles. There was a hole in his throat with a metal tube in it. The nurse explained.

"We had to do an emergency tracheotomy. He was dying. That saved his life."

The old man lay on his back unable to speak. He stared up at me. His face was a mask of fear. He knew he had problems and facing them was beyond his ability. I bent over him, looked him straight in the eye and spoke with all the authority I had.

"Now you listen to me, old man. You don't have any choice now but to listen. Whether you want to or not, you're going to hear about how God loves you. You're going to hear about my friend Jesus."

I spent the next five minutes telling him just that. Then I said, "Now, because I love you and God loves you, I'm going to pray for you, pray for your soul and pray for your body."

And, I did. Before I left, I promised I'd be back in a couple of days.

When I got back, he was still in ICU. But, the trachea tube was gone and his throat was sewn up. He could talk. He saw me coming and smiled, beaming broadly. I took that as a good sign.

"Hey, everybody," he said to the room in general, "I want you to meet my good friend Buddy. Buddy, I'm so glad to see you again. Thanks for coming."

God does work in mysterious ways.

Story Eight
Isabel

▼

Church had just ended for the morning. We were all standing around enjoying the fellowship. We were a small but close group, a group that shared a friendship born of a mutual love for the Lord Jesus. Back in the office, the phone rang. Robbie ran in and answered it. He came back into the auditorium.

"Fred, it's for you."

"Who is it?"

"A lady. She said she was a friend of your daughter."

Fred went in to answer the phone. He came out shortly.

"Come on, Elvira. We got to go."

"Problem, Fred?" I asked.

"My daughter, Isabel. She's attempted suicide. She's at the hospital."

We all knew Isabel. She wasn't Fred's biological daughter. She had been one of the two children Elvira had already had when she and Fred married. But, he treated her like his own, loved her as though he were her physical father. Isabel had attended the church on occasion but wasn't a member. Unlike the other people in the family, she denied any need for personal salvation. The whole family had at one time been nominal Catholics. Under the influence of a Baptist pastor, they had all come to accept Jesus personally and were baptized, all except Isabel.

"I've got all the religion I need," she used to tell me. We were good friends, but that's as far as she intended it would go. I'd never be her pastor.

Fred and Elvira rushed off. The rest of the group took time out to pray. We knew that Fred was both a compassionate and a proud man. It hurt him for anyone to know there were problems in his family. The others in the group overlooked that fault, knowing that in spite of the couple's love of God, all was not well within their family.

That afternoon, I rode over to their house. Elvira let me in.

"You want to tell me about it ?" I asked.

I knew they were both rather private people. But, in the time I had been their pastor, we had become close enough for them to open up to me.

"It's Isabel, "she said, "She's attempted suicide again."

"Again?" I asked.

"Yes, it's the third time she's done it."

"So what happened today?"

"Same as before. She took a bunch of pills, then got scared that it was going to work and she called her friend and told her. Her friend was who called the church. She also called the paramedics. By the time we got home, they were here and were leaving with her for the hospital."

The next day, Isabel was transferred from the hospital to the county psychiatric unit. They kept her for a while, then sent her home with a bottle of pills. I personally thought that was a strange way to treat anyone who had a habit of attempting suicide by taking pills.

Not long after that incident, I moved from that church down to Arizona to pastor. One day Fred called.

"Buddy, Isabel's in the psychiatric unit again. She's in really bad shape this time, says she wants to die. The doctors aren't able to do her any good at all. She says she wants to talk to you, if there's any way you can come to see her. She thinks you can help her."

"Sure, Fred. We'll make a combination trip. Tell her I'll be there in a couple of days. Tell Elvira I'll bring my family and we'll visit together for a few days."

"That'll be great."

Our plane got to San Francisco in the evening. Fred picked us up.

"Isabel has arranged for you and her to have a private consultation room at the hospital like the ones where the patients consult with the doctors. She's expecting you at one o'clock tomorrow."

At one the next afternoon, I met Isabel at the locked entrance to the psychiatric ward. The attendant let me in. We went to the consultation room. We sat in chairs facing each other. It has always been my habit to not have a desk between me and anyone I counsel.

"Isabel, where do you want to start?"

"A long ways back, Buddy. I want you to know why I keep feeling this need to die. It started several years ago. One night I was walking to the bus stop near our house. I was going to see a friend. On the way to the bus stop, a man forced me into his car, took me out and raped me. Until that time, I had always had a good self image. After that, I developed a negative view of myself. I began to see me as a totally unworthy individual, worthless, absolutely worthless."

The pain of remembering that awful experience showed in her face. It was not easy to sit and watch this lady I considered my friend as she talked about what had changed her life for the worse and sent her on a downward road of self-hate.

"About two years later, it happened again. I just gave up trying. I had no meaning to myself. I kept living off and on with this one man, a Greek who owns a restaurant. I knew he was just using me but that was OK. I was just using him. He has money, a good business and prestige. Living with him gives me a good feeling about myself. But then, I think how immoral it is and it sends me back down again. It's not a good relationship. We aren't in love. I probably think more of him than he does of me. Anyway, I just see me as someone who is worthless, who has no right to live."

The conversation continued in that vein for more than half an hour. Before me I saw a defeated human. The look on her face told me that she had to have some way out of this mental situation. I saw it as a spiritual problem, one that I believed could be answered by a relationship directly to Jesus. Hiding behind her supposed relationship to Catholicism was doing her no good. Her relationship to the man she lived with part-time was doing no good. Everywhere she had sought answers, she had found only more feelings of rejection.

"Isabel, look at me. Now listen closely. You need an answer. Here's what it is. We've been talking. I want you to start talking to Jesus just the way you have been talking to me. He's here, right in this room. Tell him all you've told me. Tell him what's happened and how you feel. Give it all to him. Tell him that any sin you have committed, you are sorry for and now repent of. Then, ask him to come into your heart, become part of your life and be your savior. Commit yourself to him by faith, holding back nothing."

I looked at her face, twisted with pain and covered with tears. There was a darkness over it that was inhuman, a spiritual darkness from deep within her soul.

Isabel looked upward just slightly, as though she were seeing someone just to the side of my head.

"Jesus, I want to tell you how it is with me."

She started for the first time to tell Jesus what her life had been like. I sat and listened, watching her face. As she talked, a change began to come over her. It began at the top of her head and worked downward. The wrinkles disappeared from her forehead. The tension around her eyes relaxed. A calmness began to come in her eyes which turned into a sparkle. The edges of her lips began to show faint traces of a smile. Her shoulders, which had been drawn up tight, loosened as calm relaxation spread over her body. I watched a transformation come over her physically as the same transformation came over her soul.

She talked to God for about twenty minutes. In that time, Isabel became a different person. There was a newness about her, a change, a life that dwelt within her that had not been there before. It was marvelous. It was truly miraculous.

Isabel finished what she was saying to Jesus, then looked at me again.

"Buddy, I'm so relieved, so happy. It feels so good, I don't know what I feel."

"That's OK. Just let it have complete control. Go ahead and feel good. Enjoy it."

In a few minutes she said, "Let's go talk to Mom and Dad."

The doctors saw such a change in Isabel that they let her check herself out of the hospital the next day, this time with no pills.

All's well that ends well, right? I wish that were always true.

Three years later, I got another phone call from Fred.

"Isabel's dead," he said. He was the saddest I had ever known him to be. "The funeral is tomorrow."

"Fred, I can't come right now. I'll be over to see you next week."

I knew there would be a lot of sympathetic people around for the funeral who would disappear right after the service leaving Fred and Elvira quite alone in their sadness.

About a week after the funeral, I arranged to be able to go to see my friends. It was a truly sad occasion for the three of us. They told me that Isabel had gone back to live with her Greek friend again. After a few months there, she became sad, getting more depressed each day. One day, she went back to the psychiatrist. He gave her a large bottle of pills. She went home and took them all. When the Greek came home, she was dead.

The second day I was there, Fred and I took a long drive down the coast. I drove, at his request. He was uptight, tense, nervous. I knew what the answer had to be. I asked him, "Fred, how much have you actually grieved since Isabel died?"

"None."

"No crying; no emotion?"

"No."

"What about Elvira?"

"Oh yes, she's cried-showed lots of emotion."

"Why didn't you?"

"I'm not supposed to. I need to be strong."

"Wrong, Fred. It's OK for you to cry. I encourage it. Why don't you just do that right now."

There was no noise. The tears just began slowly to run down his cheeks. Then, he began to sob.

"Oh, Buddy, I loved her so much, so much. I'm so sad, Buddy, so unhappy."

"Keep crying, Fred. Let go all your feelings."

He cried all the way home.

The next morning, I got bad news. I got up early. Fred was in the living room alone, kneeling before the easy chair praying. I watched his hands shaking and saw him cry as he prayed.

"What's wrong, Fred?"

"Buddy, I make my living as a welder. I can't afford to retire. But, I've got Parkinson's disease. I can't hold a welding rod steady enough to weld a bead. If God doesn't heal me, I'll be out of a job."

The next time I heard from the family it was four years later. Elvira called. I knew from the sound of her voice there was problems.

"Buddy, Fred died a while back. I'm alone. I have terminal cancer. I'll be dead before the month is over."

"Shall I come to see you?"

"No. Just pray for me. I'll soon be in Heaven with the others. Goodbye, Buddy."

That's the last I ever heard.

Sad story? Just remember, they were all born again believers. There is a happy ending in eternity.

There's one other little detail of Fred and Elvira's life that I thought you'd like reading about. When they got married, on the first payday, Fred brought his paycheck home and gave it to Elvira. He gave her one stipulation. All bills must be kept current. He'd make the money. She'd pay the bills. It worked out well. She did a good job of managing the finances.

Each Friday, Fred gave her the check. Each Friday, she gave him a five dollar weekly allowance. And, how do you think he squandered that princely sum? He saved every cent, every week, till Christmas time and used it to buy her a present. I think he really loved her.

STORY NINE
WATTS MIRACLES

▼

It was destined that something unusual was going to happen in the Watts family. They were ordinary people, yet there was something extraordinary about them. Let me begin where it began for me.

I had just moved to a new town to began pastoring. Early every morning I was awakened by the sound of a neighbor hammering on his roof. Every evening when I sat down to eat, the same neighbor was up on his roof pounding. I went out to look. He was putting new shingles on his house. I decided that if someone didn't help him, I was going to be listening to him for a month. I got my equipment and climbed up on his roof to help.

That action, selfish on my part, was seen as unselfish on his part. He told his neighbor, Jack Watts. As it happened, Jack and his wife Donna were in a time of spiritual searching. After talking to their neighbor, they called me to come to their house for a visit. Not too many people with no affiliation to a church invite the new preacher to their house for spiritual counseling.

I met Jack , Donna and their son Bud. That night they told me about their daughter who had died the previous year at Christmastime. She was afflicted with a disease that deteriorated his spinal cord just where it entered the neck. When it finally snapped in two she died. Her death devastated the rest of the family. They were not looking forward to the coming Christmas season. Right now they were still having a hard time dealing with her passing.

What set the daughter apart was the fact that she was the only Christian believer in the family. She'd been a member of a local Baptist church, a very devoted member. She had faced her death bravely. It presented her with no real problem.

On top of dealing with her death, there was Jack's personal problem—he was going blind. Jack was a victim of juvenile diabetes. That usually leads to disastrous results in the forties. That's where Jack was and blindness was closing in. He'd already been put on disability retirement and begun to see specialists.

That night, Jack and Donna made Jesus their lord. The following Sunday, it was my pleasure to baptize both of them. This led to one immediate positive result. The depression over the death of their daughter was lifted.

Soon began the trips to the big city to see the specialists, take tests and go to the hospital for operations. It was all an attempt to stave off the inevitable. Nothing was going stop it. Even with all the efforts, little by little, Jack's eyes failed him.

Just as blindness set in, another disaster came in Jack's life. Donna decided she could not spend her life caring for an invalid. She moved out and filed for divorce. Few times have I ever seen anyone so badly hurt as Jack was.

One thing saved him—the loving care of his family. Especially important was his brother Tim. Tim came to see Jack daily. Jack was the older and had always been loved and admired by his younger brother. Everyone in the world would be much better off if there were more brothers like Tim.

Jack's blindness was soon complete. I stopped by to see him often. About once a week, we'd go out to lunch. It amazed me how positive he was about his situation. He was always smiling; always laughing. He made friends with other handicapped people around town and spent time encouraging them. It was the days of the CB radio craze. Jack got one as a way of widening his circle of friends. Life went on. Life was OK. Life was now a continuing search for ways to help others, those Jack considered less fortunate. When I started a new radio program featuring interviews with positive people, Jack was the on the first program.

Could Jack withstand another disaster? He got one. His father, Lawson, was hospitalized due to a massive stroke. Lawson had dropped out of church years before, but he'd never dropped out of believing. Now, lying in the hospital bed, he looked bad, real bad. Of course, Jack couldn't tell that. He just knew that Lawson was sick, deadly sick.

Tim came by regularly to pick up Jack and take him to the hospital to see Lawson. One day Jack walked into the ICU and took hold of the rail on Lawson's bed. When his hand touched the rail, he spoke to Lawson, "Dad, I see you."

His dad was alert enough to question what he heard, "What are you talking about, Jack?"

Tim stood across the bed, a questioning look on his face.

"Dad, I see you," Jack said and gave the two of them a complete, detailed description of the room, the bed, the monitors, the IVs and the way Lawson's face was all distorted on the right side as a result of the stroke. The other two men were astounded at what they were hearing. They had no choice but to admit that his description was correct. Apparently Jack had been suddenly and miraculously cured of his blindness.

The weird thing was that as soon as Jack turned loose of the bed and turned to leave, he was blind again. The miracle only worked at his father's bedside. But, it happened every time he was at Lawson's bedside for exactly the amount of time he stood holding the rail.

Lawson got worse. He had been transferred to a regular room but as his condition worsened the doctors said there was no need to put him back in ICU. It wouldn't help. So he lay in the bed, in a coma, silent, eyes closed, right side of his face totally distorted.

One afternoon, knowing that the end was near, the whole family was gathered by the bed. Lawson opened his eyes, gazing intently upward. He was seeing something no one else saw. He raised his arms as if in greeting. The distortion on his face disappeared. For the first time in months, his face was normal. He smiled, a most happy smile as if in joyful anticipation. Then, he dropped backward on the bed, dead. The family was caught up in a mixture of sadness and joy.

Jack never physically saw anything on Earth again. He did receive a sort of spiritual sight. He began to walk through his house for an hour and more at a time, speaking in tongues, praying, feeling extremely happy.

One morning, Jack went into his bathroom to shave. Standing there, he had a heart attack. The paramedics said he was dead before he hit the floor. He went that quick.

After the funeral, Jack's mom, Sadie, and Tim asked me what they should put on his tombstone.

My only possible reply was, "Once I was blind, but now I can see."

STORY TEN
RUSSIAN PRISON

▼

This story contains no miracles, nothing exciting—it's a slice of life taken from a missionary journey. After the collapse of the Soviet Union my old friend Tom Cox began taking annual evangelistic trips to Russia. In 1993, I went with Tom and a group of volunteers. When I got home, I wrote this story about the happenings of two afternoons. I simply titled it 'Russian Prison Story.'

We were on the steppes of southwestern Russia, twenty miles out in the countryside south of the administrative city of Orel. The name is Russian for 'eagle'. It was cold, with a temperature in the forties Fahrenheit. The wind was blowing enough to be uncomfortable and it was raining. It was a typical midsummer day for the area. The month was June.

There were eight of us traveling together in a twelve passenger van. It had been made during the Soviet Union days in a Russian factory in Latvia. It was a 'Latvia' van. There was Gena, the young Russian who was our main driver and his associate Viktor. The other Russian was our interpreter, Mikhail, a young Muscovite who had learned English while attending college in a small town in central California.

We were five Americans, ranging in age from thirty-five to seventy-two. Wilma, the oldest, was a retired California real estate agent who spent her time traveling into the hinterlands of countries all over the world. Her friend and neighbor Arnie was a businessman who just had to get away every so often.

Frank, the youngest and the group's lead singer, was a self-employed contractor from the mountains of North Carolina. His friend Judy lived in the same town he did. These people had been teamed up by Tom with me as their leader on a trip where we lived in the homes of the Russians and saw life from their point of view.

On such a summer day, some heat in the van would have been nice. Too bad the heater did not work. Thankfully, the windshield wipers did. We needed them. Gena had turned off the highway and was headed northeast on a dirt road. He skillfully avoided the heaviest areas of mud, as much as was possible. Since this was an access road to a federal prison, there was a little better than usual maintenance on it. That means there was enough gravel to keep it passable.

We passed what we called a 'Russian pickup', a two-wheeled, rubber-tired cart pulled by a horse. The driver smiled and waved. We got the same friendliness from the people who were walking along the road.

In a few miles we came to a small river. There was an old, small, barely-adequate bridge. A hundred feet downstream a new bridge had been begun sometime in the past.

It looked as though there had been no progress on it in a long time. The bridge we were on was one lane, wood and had no side rails. It was covered in slick mud.

On a small shelf of land on the leading side of the stream was a small herd of cows, most of which were munching on the abundant green grass. A man and a woman were milking two of the cows. We assumed they would get around to all of them before darkness came.

At the edge of the water, a boy stood holding a fishing pole. He looked up as we passed, smiled and waved. Unusually friendly, these country folks. I wondered what kind of fish might be in the stream and what kind of luck he was having.

The driver of a large truck from the prison down the road waited for us to get across the bridge so he could go in the direction from which we had come. The prison was our destination this afternoon.

As we neared it, we passed a village that the road bypassed. It was home to the local farmers and to the prison workers. The tallest building was the Russian Orthodox Church, whose steeple stood above all the other buildings. A small road leading from the main road into the village carried walking people and some 'Russian pickups'.

Going up the hill east of the village, we could see the prison. First, to the right, there was the main compound with the gray wall around it that looked about thirty feet tall. To the left there were other buildings that looked like some sort of factory and some storage. Crops grew in the surrounding fields, mostly potatoes and wheat.

Gena stopped the van in front of the main building. He and Viktor went inside. Mikhail, whose nickname was Misha, explained that they were going in to try to get permission for us to visit and maybe meet some of the prisoners.

Our friends were gone about twenty minutes. When they got back, the news was bad and good. No, we could not go in today but, yes, we could tomorrow. That sounded like a real experience; a visit to the 'Gulag'.

Following the road as we had been going took us around the factory and storage buildings, past some fields, alongside the river, and eventually back to the paved road which took us to Orel.

The next afternoon, at exactly the appointed time, we were in the van parked in front of the main door of the prison. The tall walls were gray, cold-looking and depressing. There was an entry for trucks. Alongside it was a door. Between us and the two entrances was a guard shack. The two soldiers on duty were heavily armed.

Again, we waited in the van while Gena and Viktor went inside. Soon they returned with a lady who was dressed in a uniform like the guards wore. She looked us all over, asking our Russian friends questions about each of us and apparently getting satisfactory answers.

She lead the group past the guard shack and into the doorway. That put us inside the building, where we immediately entered a steel cage. It was about eight feet tall. three feet wide and twelve feet long. It was made of steel slats about a quarter of an inch thick and an inch wide, spaced four inches apart. We were completely surrounded by the cage. There was a door at the other end.

We were instructed to look to the left. There armed guards sat behind a low counter inspecting us. We all had to hold up our passports. A guard came by and examined them. When he was satisfied, he gave a signal to the guard who unlocked the inner door. We went through it single file.

Three feet past that door, we came to the exit door. It opened to a real surprise. The first thing I saw was the flowers. There were flowers everywhere. They were blooming and beautiful. The prison itself was a square of buildings around a courtyard. The courtyard had a central concrete walkway running its length next to a driveway which led from the truck entry. Off that walk, others ran to doorways set every so often in the buildings.

Everything else was covered with flowers. Here and there female prisoners cared for them. Against this backdrop, the lady commandant waited for us, along with a male assistant. There were now three officials in the group who were to lead our tour and explain us to the prisoners.

The officials, like the guards, wore army-type uniforms. I asked Misha about that and learned that they were in a military unit similar to the national guard in America. Most of them lived in the nearby village.

The prisoners wore ordinary type clothing, mostly dresses, sweaters, flat shoes and scarves. In Russia, even in summer, some sort of headgear is needed against the cold. Most women prefer scarves.

Our tour leaders were friendly, smiling and apparently glad to see us. They led us into the courtyard, explaining things as we went. It was OK to talk to the prisoners, who were friendly and happy to see us. Each of us was given flowers, fresh cut by the one presenting them.

We took a walkway over to the east side of the building, entered a door and found ourselves in a hallway about ten feet long. At the end was a stairway going up. We went to it and up.

At the first landing, I looked into the door opening to the right. There was a large barracks-like room. It was lined on either side with cots, each of which had an army blanket, sheet and pillow. Everything was neat, military-style and clean. The wooden floor appeared to not have even a speck of dust on it. There were pictures on the walls and flowers in vases. Prisoners were at work. No one was sitting or standing still.

At the next landing, we entered a door to a dayroom. It was large enough to hold comfortably about two dozen people. A small table in the center of the back wall held flowers in a vase. The room was lined with chairs. Some women were there, seated, waiting. Our group entered and took designated seats at the front, facing the prisoners.

There was a respect among the prisoners for the three officials who moved around with an ease that said they had no doubt that they were in charge. Yet, their authority wasn't flaunted. They were perfectly at ease, seated next to their charges.

In a few minutes, the room was full and overflowing with prisoners who had come to see the visiting Americans. I'm not sure if it was curiosity or seeking a diversion from the prison routine, but they came, filling the entry and flooding over into the adjacent hallway.

The commandant, who was tall, blond and really sharply dressed in her uniform, addressed the group, introducing us. Then Misha spoke for us. Turning to us, he told us that we would now sing for the prisoners.

We did a couple of songs, then did the last one in Russian, followed by doing it again with the audience joining in. They smiled, laughed and clapped in approval. Their smiles revealed a plethora of bad teeth.

Next, Frank did a couple of solos. He was young and good-looking enough to be attractive to women of all ages. He was also personable and had a great voice. They loved him. The other group members gave brief talks and were well accepted.

Then, it was my turn. Misha said they wanted to hear about America. I talked briefly, then gave them a chance to ask questions. They had plenty of them. At the end, it was necessary for the assistant commandant to call time to end the session.

As we left the room, all the ladies wanted to shake hands and speak to us individually, even though it was obvious we didn't understand them. Just the fact of speaking to us seemed important to them.

Just as I reached the doorway, a skinny, frail-looking lady whom I took to be in her sixties slipped a note into my hand and quickly turned away. I put it into my pocket. Some of the group followed us down the steps and into the yard.

We walked to the next building, and upstairs to the dayroom. Here the crowd was already packed in. We barely had a path by which to enter. It quickly closed in behind us with anxious, curious ladies.

We went through basically the same routine as before. This crowd seemed overall younger and a bit more enthusiastic. The paintings on the wall were by prisoners. Someone there had real talent. They had potted plants which showed careful and skillful handling. I commented on both. They loved it. It was like someone really cared for them individually.

With Misha's help, I led them in a question and answer discussion time. Again it got so lively that it was necessary to cut it off in order to end it. Half the crowd followed us out the door.

In the yard, they rushed off cutting fresh roses and presenting them to us. Among the Russians, a presentation of roses is a showing of honor. We were truly honored. They heaped roses upon us.

Getting out was easier than getting in. We skipped the cage. This time the guards at the counter were friendly. The commandant and her assistants accompanied us to the exit and gave us a warm goodbye.

Outside it was still cold and rainy. We still had to stomp through mud to get to the van. Sitting in it and looking out at the walls, they now seemed less cold, foreboding and depressing-just gray.

As we went down the dirt road, past the potato and wheat fields, I asked Misha to interpret the note I had gotten from the old lady. It said she had been there forty seven years and still had three more to go. Misha explained that in Russia's maximum security prisons, such as this one, there is no parole. You serve the full sentence.

The note asked if it would be possible for me to get any medical supplies to the prison. She, and others, were sick, and there were no medical supplies. Misha explained that such supplies were not available in the country. Like other things that people asked us for, they would have to be brought in from outside.

We speculated on the old lady, about why she might have been there, what crime she had committed at such a young age to earn her a life in that cold place and about how bad it must have been under communist tyranny.

Just thinking about her gave me a real need to see the sun come out. I got the answer to that metaphorically. In the front seat, Viktor and Gena started singing a stirring Russian song that lit me up inside. The good mood lasted all the way to Orel.

That's the story as I wrote it soon after coming home. For this book, I want to make an addition. The Russian man in charge of all we did on that trip was named Pyotr Kravchuk. His first name is the equivalent of Peter. He was one of the most marvelous, happiest people I ever met in any country. He was talented and a man with a great natural ability for leadership.

One would never have known, watching him, that he had spent two and a half years in prison under the Soviet regime for the crime of baptizing converts to Christianity. Of course, it was a family thing. His father and brother both served time for the same crime.

Pyotr's position was somewhat like that of a bishop, with several churches and pastors under his supervision, although in his denomination his was more of a position of caring and helping than supervising. We visited several of his churches. At one, I was told a story.

There was a small village which, under the Soviets, had been the center of a large collective farm. The people lived in the village and different ones worked the separate sections. Some grew wheat. Some were responsible for potatoes, and so on. When the Soviet Union failed, the people of that village decided that the system worked for them, so they just kept on being a co-operative with everyone working as they had before. The big difference was that now they did it voluntarily.

They had a couple of years of bad harvests and the people of the village were becoming discouraged. Bad harvests meant a lower food supply and less to sell to bring in cash. They needed to do something. A big change had to come. During the third planting season, Pyotr was in the village visiting the local church. The people had an idea. They'd ask him to pray for the crop.

They asked him. He agreed. He gathered into a group as many of the people as were willing and able to be present. That included almost everyone. He prayed, in great faith, believing that God would hear. Because of his faith, the people confidently believed.

Did it work? They had the best harvest in the more than fifty year history of the collective, by far better than ever before. Practically everyone in the village decided that with those kind of benefits, they needed to be Christians. The local congregation grew swiftly. God does indeed hear and answer.

Story Eleven
The Tragedy Called Life

$$\blacktriangledown$$

Things looked good for Terry Green. He had a good job in the oilfields. That gave him the ability to support his family. It was a nice family; a loving wife and two sons, aged sixteen and twelve. They had a nice home to live in. Yes, he was satisfied and happy. As far as he knew, the other three members of his family were also satisfied and happy. He also had some good friends, men he had met around town and men he worked with, good men; men he enjoyed knowing and spending time with.

He never did know what caused the problems to start. All he could tell me was that they did. But, it seemed like once they were begun it was like a river, couldn't be stopped. Now, remember, like all the stories in this book, this one is true. I did change Terry's name.

It all started one afternoon at home. Terry was watching TV. His wife Janet was in the kitchen and the two boys were both in their rooms. Suddenly, the peaceful atmosphere of the afternoon was shattered by the sound of a gunshot, like a rifle. The sound came from the oldest boy's bedroom. Terry, Janet and the other son all came running at once. Terry kicked open the door and saw nothing, just the furniture, no son.

He walked over to the bed and looked behind it. There between the bed and the wall lay the body of his son. In his hand was a .22 caliber rifle. There was a hole in the top of his head. He'd put the gun in his mouth and fired. There was no note. No one had any idea what was wrong. Life was not so good any more.

Soon after they buried their son, Janet turned to drugs. She was filled with sadness and just couldn't face life. The drugs seemed to help. The problem was the cost. Her friendly neighborhood pusher, who operated from a house near two schools, offered her a suggestion. She could become a dealer. She accepted the idea without hesitation. Now, she could afford her habit.

Being an amateur in a small town, it was only a short time till she got arrested. The judge gave her five years in the county women's prison.

Terry was left at home with his young son. It wasn't easy being the provider, father and substitute mother for a boy just turning teenager. Terry tried. He also took up drinking. In a couple of months he lost his job. That left no money for house payments. A couple more months and the house was gone.

Here we now have an unemployed, drinking father of a young son who has no place to live except the local transient hotel, which is full of dopers and drinkers. You guessed it. Word swiftly got to child protective services. They took Terry's son.

He was fortunate that the local oilfield contractors needed occasional day help. He managed to pick up about half-time work that way. It paid for the hotel, food and alcohol. Still, he had friends. That helped.

What else could go wrong? One afternoon, a warm summer day, a man who worked in the oilfields with Terry went up on the hill outside of town, removed his pants, took out a pocket knife and severed his sex organs. Then he sat on a rock and bled to death. That evening when the police found his body, there was a note beside it requesting that 'since I don't know any preachers, I want my friend Terry Green to speak at my funeral.'

Somehow, Terry worked up the strength to carry out the request. He later told me that it was about the hardest thing he'd ever done.

So far, it must appear that this story has no plot. You're right. I'm simply reciting to you the tragedies of a real-life, modern day Job. There's more.

One night, not long after his friend's funeral, Terry was sitting in the bar across the street from the hotel. He got to talking to a man in there, just a friendly conversation. The man was new in town, come in to try to find work in the oilfields. By the time the evening was over the man had spent what few dollars he had and was left with nothing with which to pay for a room.

"That's OK," Terry said, "My room has a double bed. You can sleep with me. Tomorrow you can go to where I work. Maybe they'll need a man for a day."

They went to the room where each climbed into his side of the bed. Due to the amount of drinking they had done, both were asleep almost instantly. The next morning, when the alarm went off, Terry, hungover as usual, awoke and shook his new friend. The man was dead, stone cold dead. He had apparently died soon after they went to sleep. Terry had spent the night sleeping with a corpse. Now that had to be explained to the police. It also cost him a day's work.

After all this, Terry really began to think he was a jinx or that he was jinxed. But, there's more. The oilfield contractor he worked part-time for stopped needing regular help. That left Terry without money to even pay for the hotel room. He told James, one of his drinking buddies, about it.

"Hey, come on down and stay at our house with us, man. No problem."

The only problem was that it was a six room house with one bath and when Terry got there he made a total of nine men living there. But, it was a place to sleep. Maybe things would begin to turn around.

One of the nine men living in the house was James' father. He was a long-term heavy drinker. His wife had divorced him a few years before because of his habit. About a month after Terry moved in, the old man got totally dehydrated and died right there in his bed. I was the ex-wife's pastor. The family asked me to do the funeral.

I had already been to the house a few times attempting to minister to the men there. After the funeral, Terry asked me to go with him to the county prison to visit his wife. On the trip over and back, he told me this story. Sad, but true.

Is that all? Not quite. Two months later James died in jail. He was picked up for public drunk and died in his sleep. The cause was cirrhosis of the liver brought on by years of heavy drinking.

There was no longer anyone to be responsible for the rent on the house. The seven men living there scattered. I never saw or heard from Terry again. That was seventeen years ago. I've often wondered.

Like I said, this story had no plot, didn't even have a moral. It just how life is sometimes.

For a related story see 'Attempting To Overcome'.

STORY TWELVE
GOD THE HEALER AT WORK

▼

Twice I had been asked to preach in a church in Rusk, a small town in east Texas. This church was unusual in the fact of a being a charismatic Baptist group. They were definite believers in the idea of the Spirit of God being at work in a powerful way among Christians in the present day. Their beliefs were being justified as they saw things happening among their people that were not of normal human or scientific explanation.

The present pastor was a friend of mine whose name was Jerry. He asked me to return to the church to be the speaker for the homecoming day services. We would have the morning worship service, a potluck dinner, then an afternoon service, which would be mainly singing. It was a pleasure I looked forward to.

When I arrived on Saturday afternoon, Jerry and I rode together to the church. He explained to me some difficulties that had arisen in the area of sickness.

"To begin with, Buddy, my wife is sick. She has something like flu. It's been going around. She's been at home sick for four days, I mean really bad sick. That means that she won't be here. Next, whatever she's got, I'm beginning to come down with. It started today. I've been getting worse by the hour. If it works out for me like it did for her, I'll be too sick by morning to come to church. You'll have to take charge of it all. The people will understand. Last, there's Brother Elliot. You know how much he likes you and I know you consider him a good friend. Probably he will not be here."

"What's his problem?"

"It's his back. About three weeks ago, he got down in his back and he's been in bed ever since. He's in great pain; taking a lot of pain pills but still hurting. He only gets out of bed to go to the doctor. No way he can be here tomorrow."

"I'm truly sorry to hear about his problem. Maybe we can get by there and pray for him tomorrow afternoon."

"Like I said, I may not even be here. You'll have to go alone."

"No. We're not going to accept the idea of you not being here. Let's pray right now, asking God to heal you and believing in his power for you and your wife. We need you in the service tomorrow and you both need to be well."

Feeling the leadership of the Spirit of God, I put my hand on his forehead and prayed that he would be relieved of his sickness and that his wife would be raised up from her bed and made whole.

"Thanks, Buddy," he said, "I hope that has some effect on me. Right now I feel so bad I'm having a hard time believing it will."

"That's OK. I'll see you here in the morning,"

When I arrived at the church at ten the next morning, there was Jerry, all bright-eyed and happy, looking and feeling great.

"How's your wife?" I asked.

"Still in bed."

"You made it; keep believing on her behalf."

Just at time for the service to start, in came our dear friend, Brother Elliot. He was bent over double from the back problem. Standing as straight as he could his eyes were focused directly on the floor below him. It was a pity to see that wonderful man in such a state, yet encouraging to see that he had worked up the determination and strength to be able to get to the church. No doubt, it was a great effort on his part.

When the singing and greetings had ended, it was time for me to deliver the message. When I got up, I felt a definite leadership of God to deviate briefly from my plan. Following God's leadership, I called Brother Elliot to the front. He got up from his seat, evidently in much pain. Slowly, he made his way to where I was, his face pointed toward the floor.

When he reached me, I put my hand on his head and said, "Let's pray. Lord, we come to you on behalf of this dear brother. Heal him, we ask you in the name of Jesus. Amen."

Slowly, Elliot began to straighten up. For three weeks, he'd been bent over. Now, he was getting well. His head moved from its horizontal position to the vertical. In about one minute, he was looking me in the eye, standing straight up.

"Praise the Lord," he said.

"What about the pain?" I asked.

"All gone. I feel no pain whatever."

"Thank you, Jesus."

Elliot went back to his seat a lot faster than he had come to the front. He sat down smiling-beaming with joy. I thought that now I was ready to preach. As I looked down the center aisle, there halfway back was a boy about nine years old in a wheelchair with both legs in casts. I walked back to him.

"Son, I want to pray for you," I said laying my hand on one of the casts, "I'm not going to hurt you; just ask God to help you. Lord, on behalf of this child, I ask your power to move to heal to the glory of Jesus. Amen."

I went back to the front and preached.

Before leaving to go home, I went by Jerry's house. As I followed him into the driveway, there was his wife standing on the porch, smiling and happy. During the time of the services, the sickness had suddenly left her. She felt great. The power had been at work.

The next week, I got a letter from Jerry. It was about the boy in the wheelchair. He was in the wheelchair because he had been run over by a pickup truck. Each leg had been overrun by both the back and front wheel. Both legs were broken twice. The doctor had predicted a long healing period.

According to the boy's mother, after I had prayed over the boy, he had begun to wiggle. He couldn't be still. His legs had begun to heal. Next morning, she took him to the doctor. The legs had already healed to the point of being so strong his wiggling had cracked both casts. He was going to be out running around months ahead of the medical schedule.

Four prayed for; four healed. Good average.

Story Thirteen
The Watts Preacher

▼

Everybody who has read a newspaper or seen a TV news-cast in the past thirty years knows that Los Angeles has a section called Watts. There are two things to be known about Watts. First, the population is black. Second, some of the meanest blacks in America live there, along with some of the finest ones.

Here's a fast example for you. A carpenter I knew, white man, went down to Watts in his camper to do volunteer building work for a black church. They were overjoyed to have him but at night he was locked inside a chain link fence. The people at the church cared enough to do that to him for his own protection.

This story is about another black church that was doing remodeling. They called a company in Texas that is about the biggest there is in the church remodeling busi-ness. We won't name them here to keep my publisher from getting sued. The company sent a representative to the church. One night he held a public meeting to show the pastor and the church some of the things his company had to offer.

One of the items which came up was something called crinkleglass. The salesman knew he would have a surefire hit with that, considering the location of the church. He pulled out a sample from his sales kit, sat it on the altar table and explained it something like this, "Crinkleglass is stained glass. It gives your church the beauty of stained glass when you've got that Sunday morning sun shining through. But, more important than that, it's vandal proof. They cannot throw rocks through it. It's even bulletproof. No one is going to destroy your windows or damage them in any way when you use this fine product."

The preacher got up and interrupted the salesman. "You say it's

bulletproof?", he asked.

"That's right," the salesman assured him, smiling at the congregation.

With that, the pastor pulled out a revolver from a shoulder holster and emptied six shots at the glass, hitting it every time.

"You're right," he said, "It is bulletproof."

When they got the salesman woke up from his dead faint, they gave him an order.

STORY FOURTEEN
RICHARD'S JOKE

▼

You'll soon figure out that this book is not autobiographical and not in any particular order of time and space. I just write them down as I remember them. The next one that comes to mind is my old friend Richard and a little something that happened to him in 1973.

At the time, I was living in Phoenix, Arizona with my family, attempting to do some missionary work and catching whatever came along for my family's support. I had known Richard three years. He lived at Blackwater on the Pima Indian Reservation, out in the desert southeast of Phoenix.

Richard was pastor of the Baptist church at Blackwater. All he got out of that was an old rundown house to park his family in. Not a really satisfactory situation. Even worse was the fact that he was still a student at Grand Canyon College, which was fifty miles away. He rode his motorcycle back and forth to school for gas economy but it was still a long ride.

He had attempted to find himself a paying church situation that would provide for his family and be closer to school. Now and again, he got a call to preach for a pastorless church on the possibility of being called as pastor. There seemed to be one fatal flaw in his presentation—his favorite joke.

Richard was a nice man, knew the Bible, had a good delivery-everything looked in his favor. There was no reason that none of those churches wanted him. His wife said it was that dumb joke. Richard loved that joke. He thought it was hilariously funny. His wife hated it. Oh yes, her name was-still is-Alice.

Anyway, everytime Richard got called someplace to preach, Alice said, "Don't tell that stupid joke."

He told it every time. Nobody ever even laughed-nobody. You'd have thought that might have given old Rich a clue. We don't usually take clues that make our favorite things look bad.

Meanwhile, up in Phoenix, the Twenty-Second Avenue Baptist Church was without a pastor and I was filling in. I had no real interest in making it a permanent situation for myself. But, I got to thinking about Richard. It was ideal.

There was a house, just barely big enough for his family and it sat right in the churchyard, which meant no expense to get to work. It was two miles from the college; no expense to get to school. The church paid the utilities and it even had a phone. You couldn't get a phone out at Blackwater. Add to all that the fact that it was OK for him to be a student and they would pay him thirty-five dollars a week.

I told the church about Richard. They picked a Sunday morning for him to come preach for them. I arranged it with him.

At the house in Blackwater that Sunday morning, as the family was preparing for church, Alice was emphatic, "Do not tell that stupid joke."

Richard, as usual, was offended.

At eleven-thirty, looking splendid all dressed up in suit and tie, black leather Bible in hand, Richard stepped to the pulpit and began his delivery. Alice held her breath. He did not tell the joke!!! She was ecstatic. She had no idea what Richard did say that morning. She was too busy rejoicing over what he didn't say.

They came back that night for the evening service. During the service, the church held a short business session and asked Richard to become their pastor, beginning immediately. Alice let him know quickly that there was no doubt that it was God's will for them to accept. She was tired of the exotic life out on the reservation.

They packed and moved on Monday. By Tuesday evening, Alice had the house all straight and ready for visitors. It's a good thing. The people came.

The next Sunday, there was Richard, the new pastor and all his family-Alice and the five kids-in church, on time and looking good. Alice was proud of Richard. Richard, sitting in his chair on the platform was proud of his family. The church members were all proud of their new pastor.

At eleven-thirty it was time for the sermon. Richard stepped to the pulpit and began with to speak. "Oh no," Alice's mind screamed, "He's telling that dumb joke." She cringed. She squirmed and slid down in her seat. She opened her Bible and pretended to read it. Finally, Richard reached that idiotic punchline, the part that was usually followed by a deafening silence. She held her breath.

He delivered the punchline. The whole church burst out in uproarious laughter. They loved it. Alice looked around. People were laughing extendedly at the joke. Some were crying from the effect of the mirth. Others held their sides. It was unbelievable.

Behind the pulpit, Richard smiled. He had found his home.

By the way, did you notice that I told the story, but never told the joke. I am

one of those who never thought it was funny. That's one time that I agreed with Richard's wife. That being true, I didn't want to bore you with it.

Story Fifteen
A Few More Church Laughs

▼

Now, don't get the idea that this whole book is about Richard, the guy in the last story. But, this story is. Before he went to Blackwater, he spent a short stint at the Casa Blanca Baptist Church at Bapchule, Arizona. They didn't have a house to live in. That's why he ended up at Blackwater. Well, anyhow, his friend Dan was pastor over at the Maricopa church, which was also on the reservation. They decided that one Sunday night they would hold a joint baptism service at Maricopa.

It took place in the middle of winter. You may remember the Arizona desert as hot but it does cool off in winter. You also have to remember that Baptist baptize by total immersion, which is done in a large tank of water usually built into the front of the church.

Richard had a couple of little Indian boys to baptize and he went first. When he stepped into the water, it was bone-chilling. His breath caught and it was a minute before he could breathe enough to speak. Confidently, he moved around in the waist deep water, said a few words, then motioned the first boy into the tank. Hesitantly, the kid came down the steps, then stood silently as Richard prayed over him. Then Richard laid him back into the water.

He came out with a scream and shouted, "My God, that's cold!"

He leaped for the exit steps. Richard, trying to hold his composure and look as dignified as possible, turned and motioned for the other boy who stood at the top of the entry steps, took him into the water and, with a prayer laid him back.

This one came up shouting, "Whoowee, you're right," as he leaped for the

exit steps leaving an embarrassed pastor behind.

Here's a couple of more short ones on Richard, then we'll let him rest.

These happened at the Twenty-Second Avenue Church. When I was supply preaching for them and recommended Richard, a lady asked my wife, loudly in the middle of the meeting, referring to me, "What's the matter, don't he want no church?"

We just referred to her as the red-haired lady. A little bit of what hair she had left was still red. The rest was gray. Now, keep her in mind.

I've indicated to you that, aside from that one dumb joke, Richard was a dress up dignified type of preacher. He wasn't like me. I've been known to go on round the world preaching tours and never take a tie, white shirt or dress coat. But, Richard had his dignity and wanted all things done, as the Bible says "decently and in order."

One Sunday night the church was celebrating what some churches refer to as the sacrament of communion, but which Baptists fondly call the ordinance of the Lord's Supper. It was all going just beautifully.

There the pastor stood behind the communion table presiding with his two deacons on either side of him to do the serving. With the proper scriptures and prayers, the serving of the bread was introduced, then the two deacons served the plates with the tiny pieces of bread to the congregation. Each member took a piece. At the signal they all partook together.

Then, to the juice. Baptist aren't much on wine. They use grape juice. Richard had found a bottle in the church office, apparently left from the last such service. Not having time to go to a store for a fresh bottle, he used that one, filling the little individual serving sized glasses.

Now, he removed the lid from the serving tray, again did the appropriate scriptures and prayers, then gave the trays to the deacons to serve to the congregation. Each member took one. At the signal they all raised their glasses together and drank.

The dignity of the moment was shattered by the red-haired lady shouting for all the world to hear, "Oh Lordy! That's sour!!"

Red-faced, Richard had a hard time restoring dignity and order.

Here's a couple of deacon stories. The first one will bring us to the end of our stay at Twenty-Second Avenue Church. No great punchlines to either of these. They just illustrate people.

In most Baptist churches across the country, it is a long-standing custom, vastly approved by the congregations, to have a monthly business meeting. It is usually held on the Wednesday night following the first Sunday, taking the place of the service commonly called the Wednesday Night Prayer Meeting.

The people look forward to the business meetings. It is a great example of American democracy in action. Any member present has a right to participate in whatever business comes to hand.

Here was Richard, new pastor, in his first situation that even required holding business meetings. The reservation churches didn't bother with such customs. Richard anticipated the evening with a mixture of feelings. After all, these people had been attending business meetings for years but he had never presided at one. He even called me to ask how to go about it. I just told him to read what happened at the last meeting and use that for a script. It had always worked for me.

The meeting was opened with a song, then prayer. Next, the pastor called the church into the business session. They had the reading by the church clerk of the minutes of the last meeting. This was followed by the treasurer's report, the Sunday School report and reports from the other church organizations.

With the reports out of the way, it was time for business. Someone made a motion. There was a second, followed by discussion. All this was done in such a fashion as to indicate that the people were thoroughly acquainted with Roberts' Rules Of Order, a book second only to the Bible in most Baptist churches.

A vote was called. "All in favor say 'aye'", Richard said, looking around expectantly. There was total dead silence. Every head in the house turned toward the back seat, where the chairman of deacons, Brother Jackson, sat. They looked at him and waited. He slowly nodded his head 'yes.'

Everyone turned back to the pastor and voiced a loud unanimous 'aye.'

Well, now Richard knew where all the power was and how the church ran business-wise.

One last deacon story, then off to something else. This one happened to me. Yes, this is autobiographical. In 1978, I went to Taft, California to pastor. The church had three deacons. All of them were fabulously good to me, at first. All pastors can understand that last sentence.

One of the deacons served as church treasurer and the other two alternated year by year being chairman of the board. Garlin didn't seem to care one way or the other about the honor. Wayne loved it.

On Sunday mornings, Wayne sat slightly forward of center by the window on the north side with his wife between him and the wall. He was in a position to be seen by most of the people present.

I made a habit of ending the sermon so that the people were out by noon. I knew the unpadded pews got tough on the bones of the older ones, of whom there were several. After I had been there about a year, Wayne started a new habit. Every Sunday morning at seven minutes till twelve, he lifted his left arm, moved it forward to allow his watch to be seen past his coat sleeve, bent his arm and slowly raised his arm up near his face.

He had one of those early lighted display watches that you had to mash a button on the side to light up the dial to see the time. Slowly he reached over with his right arm and mashed the button. Then, his eyes popped up as though to say, "Good Lord, is it that late already?"

Of course, he had previously snuck a peek to ascertain that it was time for his ceremony. This began to draw much attention from the crowd and greatly cut down on the attention they were paying to my summation. It got to where the people expected it and began looking toward him when showtime came. The effect of my sermons suffered. Wayne loved it. He loved the attention and the fact that it seemed that he was in control and was to be given credit for the service ending on time.

One morning, after several months of this, I watched him go through his motions one more time. Then, spontaneously, I stopped, straightened my arm, slid it forward to reveal my watch, bent my elbow and drew my wrist up to my face, staring at my watch. Then, very slowly I put it down, stared Wayne right in the eye and went back to preaching, adding five minutes.

We never had another showtime. The spell was broken.

Oh yes, one other thing about Wayne. We were good friends for a while. I can say a few good things about him. I can attest that he loved a good joke. For several years he was manager of the lumber company in Taft. One day, when business was slow, he gave one of his employees the phone number of a lady who lived up in the hilly section of town and gave him instructions what to say. It went like this.

"Hello, Mrs.—. This is Tommy with the phone company repair service. We are going to be blowing air through the phone lines to clean the dust out of them. We don't want to get your house dirty. Would you please tie a paper bag over your receiver?"

"Why, yes, I will. Thanks for calling."

The lady was a friend of Wayne's and he called her later. She did tell him that she had had the phone covered since the previous call.

STORY SIXTEEN
THE WHITE SPIDER

▼

This is not a funny story. I guess, if anything, you'd have to call it a weird story. But, I can tell you one thing for sure. It's totally true. It all happened to me. Yeah, one of those autobiographical things.

Becky, my wife, and I were living in Gainesville, Florida. She was a housewife. I was circulation manager of the local newspaper, the Gainesville Sun.

My mom and dad, Sallie and Ree Holbrook lived seventy-five miles away, on the side of Lake Harris between Leesburg and Tavares, Florida. Dad was retired, did a lot of fishing and was part-time pastor of Haines Creek Baptist Church, not far from the house.

I worked all night on Saturday and usually went home and went to bed. Well, sometimes I went to church and did my sleeping there while Earl preached. He didn't mind. One particular Sunday morning, I went home with the heaviest urge to go see my folks. As soon as I got home, we ate breakfast then headed south.

It was a fantastic visit. It was a nice, but warm, summer day. We had a good lunch, then sat and talked. Then, Dad wanted to go walking, just him and me. We wandered slowly around the yard, discussing this and that, nothing in particular. There were a few things going on in my life at the time that Dad was rather proud of and he said so; unusual for him.

I had noticed that he was doing a lot of work on his house. When I asked him about it, he said, "I'm getting it ready for your mother when I'm gone."

He talked to me and looked at me like he knew death was in his near future. But, there was no sadness, no regret. It was just totally factual, the way he would announce a routine meeting in church. Still it seemed strange, not something to worry about. He was in perfect health, never had a sick day in his life. He looked as good as I could ever remember.

We had one of the best days ever. When it was time to go home, they gave us some fresh vegetables; some from their garden, others that had been given to them. They included some ears of green corn. I laid those in the front floorboard of the car, near my feet. I was on the passenger side. Becky drove.

Near the house, we stopped for gas. Before I got out of the car, I looked down. There on top of the corn was a tiny, white spider. I was looking down on top of it. It was just over a quarter of an inch long, all white except some tiny shadowy spots on its back. It formed a perfect human skull. Really eerie. I'd never seen anything like it before and never have since.

I got the gas. When I got back in, the spider was gone.

Two weeks later, on a Sunday morning, I got that same urge again to go see the folks. This time I did not go. I slept till afternoon then we took my plane up for a relaxing ride. Before we went to bed that night, that feeling came again that I should have gone to Leesburg.

On Tuesday, it was hot: one hundred ten degrees and one hundred percent humidity. When the papers came off the press, I was out back with the carriers, checking, seeing that all was OK. Besides being hot it was noisy.

I got a phone call. It was Nell, the treasurer of Dad's church. Dad had a heart attack. They had taken him to the hospital. It was serious. I got off work, went home, called my sister in Georgia and took Becky to Leesburg.

When we got to the house, Nell let us in, only saying that Mom was in the bedroom. As I walked in and saw her, I knew Dad was dead. He had been dead when Nell called. She just had not yet known.

It went like this. Dad had gone to Elmer's house to help him mend his roof. After a while, he needed a tool that was at home in his garage. He went and got it. Remember, it was hot. After he got the tool, he went into the house and got a cold cola from the refrigerator. Sitting by the table, he drank it.

Before the drink was done, he told Mom he had a stomach ache. He went to the couch and laid down. It got worse. Mom called an ambulance. The parameds came, examined him and took him to the hospital. He was dead before they left.

I thought about the last time I had been there, the strange urges to go, the talk Dad and I had, his foreknowledge of his impending demise and about that spider. Thirty years later, I can still see that spider.

One last thing. On a hot summer day, when it's humid and I get overheated, I do not have a cold cola-not me.

STORY SEVENTEEN
OVER THE MOUNTAIN

▼

Let me tell you about my friend Ross. The last I heard from Ross, he had earned his doctorate degree, was a professor at a major university, and was part-time pastor of a church. It was no ordinary church, mind you. The way I heard it, they hold services in the Navaho Indian language, one of the most difficult languages on Earth for those not born to it. Ross has known it for years, fluently.

Ross left his hometown in the Midwest in the late forties as a very young man with a brand new wife and went to the Navaho reservation in northwestern New Mexico to be a missionary; an independent, live by faith type missionary. Not an easy life.

One of the first difficulties he ran across was the language barrier. Sure, some of the Indians spoke English, but a lot didn't. None of the missionaries spoke Navaho. Ross set out to learn it, along with all the other things there were to learn; like all the customs that were so different from what the people back home had.

Then, there was the immense size of the reservations, covering space in four states. Way back on the Navaho reservation, there was the Hopi reservation. It was a lot of space, with a lot of people and sometimes a lot of space between people.

Ross learned the language, the first white man in history to learn it fluently. He learned the land, the people and the customs. He was there to teach the people Christianity but he was there to respect who and what they already were.

Somehow, by faith, he got hold of one of those old Dodge vans that were available back in the fifties, nothing like the ones today. He began running up the mileage, getting to villages all over the reservation.

One day, after a long, arduous drive over the desert, he showed up in a truly remote village, surprising all the people who saw him. The first man he stopped to talk to had a question.

"Say, mister, which side of the mountain did you come around, the east or the west?"

"What do you mean?"

"Well, you came from the south, didn't you?"

"Yes, that's right."

"To get to this village from the south, you either have to go on the east or

the west side of the mountain."

"I didn't go east or west. I came over the mountain."

"You can't go over the mountain."

"Nobody told me."

And that's how Ross was about everything. There's lots of stories about him. Maybe I"ll tell more later. Right now just one.

Ross spent a bunch of years with the Indians, then he went back home and taught college, then moved to Arizona to teach college. That's where I met him. We did mission work on the Pima reservation together, you know, the same one our friend Richard lived on.

Ross had two great kids, son and daughter. He loved them both. His daughter got married to a psychologist. Life was good; or so it seemed. Ross was unaware of what was going on in his daughter's marriage.

One day she came home, in tears, a total wreck. The truth was, the marriage had been a shambles since the day the honeymoon ended. From the daughter's description, her psychologist husband was a bit of a nut case himself.

Everyday it was a matter of living with yelling and screaming, constant negative put-downs, unbelievable verbal abuse. She was at the edge. There was no way she could take anymore. It finally came to the breaking point the previous evening. The husband forced her to sit down on the side of the bed. Then he sat beside her and yelled in her ear, very abusive, for one hour.

She cried through the telling. Ross got hotter by the second. We're talking about a normally easy going, quiet man who would never get angry, never dream of hurting anyone. But, that was his daughter sitting there in tears, tears brought by a husband who acted like no man ever should.

Ross got in his pickup and went to their house. Once inside he was very straight-forward with his son-in-law.

"I'm going to tell you this one time. I know what you've been doing to my daughter. It stops today. If you find that difficult to live with, think of this. I have lots of friends on the reservation, primitive friends who don't live by white mens' standards. These people would be glad to do me a favor. They know ways to physically abuse people that you have never imagined. Do you think you can understand what I'm talking about?"

The message was swiftly sinking into the young man's head. He nodded, unable to speak.

"If my daughter ever again tells me that you have abused her in any manner, I will immediately call some friends to come visit you. Remember that."

With that, he left. But, he left an impression. The daughter went back home to her husband, a very loving, kind, gracious man. I never again heard of them having any problems. It don't take some guys' imagination long to figure out how things should be.

STORY EIGHTEEN
MANUEL THE MAYO

▼

Most folks have heard of the Maya (ends in 'a') Indians of Mexico. Most donot know that there is a Mayo (ends in 'o') tribe. The Maya live on the southeast side of Mexico, near the Gulf of Mexico. The Mayo live in the northwest coast, next to the Pacific Ocean.

My friend Manuel was a Mayo. If you go south on Highway 15, the west coast highway, you come to the city of Navajoa. Just south of there, off to the left is an Indian village called Bacabachi. That was where I met Manuel Fragosa.

To digress briefly, my partner Steve and I had been asked by Paul Green, a missionary, to go to this town and repair the church building which had been severely damaged by a hurricane. Paul supplied the expense money. The plan was to work all day and hold evangelistic meetings at night.

When we got there, we found one extremely discouraged Indian. The whole roof was off the building, except for the small area in the rear which served as his one room living space. The building was dirty. The congregation was down near zero.

We began to get out the message that we were holding meetings at the church with Anglos doing preaching and singing. The first day we had a few people. Then, we went to town and bought materials for construction. A few curiosity seekers came by.

There were a few items which might prove interesting to you the reader. One, the outhouse was at the edge of the yard. It had no roof, just the blue sky above, the better to dissipate odors. Some people who lived behind the church had a flock of goats. Every morning, they ran the goats through the churchyard on the way to pasture. Every evening they returned, through the churchyard. Those same folks had a rooster which crowed all night, about every fifteen minutes.

It was Easter time and in that part of Mexico, hot weather comes early in the spring. It also comes early in the day. The nights in the masonry building never really got cooled off. We slept on the ground outside seeking enough cool to be able to sleep.

Each morning, we took turns taking a bucket to the faucet at the corner to wash and shave using cold water. It was a way to start the day cool. That was followed by breakfast in the backyard of a nearby home, where the lady was contracted to feed us. If we needed materials, we got up early and had breakfast at the farmers' market in town.

The people came by regularly to see the progress on the church. We hammered, smiled, waved, shouted out what Spanish we knew, and worked on in the heat. Evenings we would wash by the faucet, eat supper with the lady, then hold services. The crowds got progressively bigger. Finally,

Steve and I had only standing room behind the concrete pulpit stand, due to kids sitting everywhere on the floor. Adults took up all the seats.

One day I was up in the rafters when my wallet dropped from my pocket landing on the floor. It was stuffed with a few hundred dollars worth of pesos. I don't think Manuel had ever seen so much money at one time in his life. He was alone on the floor, waiting to hand up materials. His eyes bulged at the sight of the fat wallet. He picked it up and raised it straight up toward me. It motioned him to put it in his pocket. I intended for him to hold it till we got down. I trusted him completely. Later, when I got down, his first action was to hand me the wallet. I did not count the money.

About the fourth day, I noticed that Manuel sang all the time and all the time it was the same song. I thought maybe it would be nice if he got a different song. Finally, I got to listening. This man who had been so discouraged just a few days ago, was singing over and over 'God Is So Good.' No need to change that.

Well, here's the point of this story. About the end of the week, on an exceedingly hot afternoon, Steve and I were on the roof, nailing down the sheets of steel roofing. The sun was reflecting off them blindingly. It must have been a hundred forty degrees up there. We paused and I looked down at Manuel who waited anxiously beside the building just far enough out to see us.

I wiped the sweat and told him how wonderful a tall, cold glass of lemonade would taste. He laughed. I knew there was no lemonade in all of Bacabachi. After a short rest, we went back to hammering.

In a little while, I noticed that Manuel was gone. Steve had not noticed him leave. Oh well, probably gone to arrange the evening meal.

After more than an hour we heard a shout from the ground. There stood Manuel, a huge smile on his face and a tall glass of icy lemonade in each upraised hand. We lost no time getting to the ground.

Here's what he had done. He looked all around his room, scraping up every last centavo he owned. He knew I had money, but this was his gift. He took all of his small money supply and walked one mile north to the only store. There he bought the only two lemons in the town. He walked half a mile east to the only bar and used the last of the money he had to buy ice. He also gave up a lot of his pastoral dignity to enter that place, it being against his principles to be there.

Manuel then walked a mile back south to the lady's house and prepared two icy glasses of lemonade and walked them the fifty yards to the church, very proudly. I think that in all my life, few drinks have held the meaning of that glass of lemonade, or been shared in better company.

The last night of the meeting the church repair was finished. The crowd was overflowing. The benches were full. The floor was full. All the windows and doors
were crowded. Manuel the Mayo was a happy man.

Story Nineteen
Dewberry Number Two

In the spring of 1962, I began to travel regularly on the Highway 129 going north out of Gainesville, Georgia. I was along there at least three trips per week, sometimes more. About the second time through, I noticed a white church building out in the country on the west side of the road with a sign over the front door that said 'Dewberry Baptist Church # 2'.

Well, that got me curious and I looked up the one man who was sure to know the story, Reverend Warren. He had been living in those hills since the late 1870s and knew everything and everybody as far as Baptist churches was concerned.

Sure, he knew the story. It goes back into the history of the Baptist movement. They were divided about equally between the Calvinists and the Arminians.

The Calvinist believed the Bible as taught by John Calvin who said that everything for everyone is predestined. That is, God decided before the creation of the Earth what everyone's destiny would be. Spiritually, that meant that God had already decided that some would be Christians and others would not, meaning that it was already decided who would go to Heaven and who would go to Hell.

The Calvinists did not hold evangelistic meetings to get folks saved, i.e., converted to Christianity. They held meetings to teach their view of the Bible. When God was ready to save someone, he would do it without any help.

The Arminians followed the teachings of Arminius who taught that people had free wills. They could decide their life and eternal destiny. They believed that Jesus meant it literally when he said, 'Whosoever will let him come and receive freely.'

This group held evangelistic meetings to encourage people to accept Jesus personally and secure their position in the kingdom of God both in this life and eternally.

It was the custom, in farming communities back about the turn of the century and on up to the twenties, to hold extended meetings in August of every year. At these meetings there would be the morning session, ending before lunch, and the evening session, after the evening meal and sometimes lasting late. There was usually a separate preacher for the day and night sessions. It was also the custom that these preachers might be of opposing theological persuasions.

At the Dewberry Baptist Church, the only one existing at that time, they were holding such a meeting. The day preacher was Calvinist and the night preacher was Arminian. Each attended the others' sessions, just to criticize, and they fought constantly about who was right. But, they had to see each other constantly because the attending members fed them their meals and they had every meal together.

During the last half of the second week, at lunchtime one day, the two preachers were eating together in a country home. Let me define that. It was a log cabin in a grove of pine trees. There was no yard as such, just a cleared out dirt spot inhabited by kids, chickens and dogs. The dogs were never far away at eating time.

The front door led to a large room that served as living room, dining room and kitchen. The table was in the middle of the room. It being summer, the doors and windows were open, trying to catch a little breeze.

The preachers and the adults of the family sat down to eat. As usual, in poor country homes, the main dish was fried chicken. After the lengthy blessing, the Calvinist preacher picked up a drumstick from the plate and pointed it at the Arminian, making a point.

"Do you see this chicken leg? Far back in eternity, long before man or the Earth were created, God predestined that I, on this date, in this place, at this table, should eat this piece of chicken."

Smiling triumphantly, his point well made, he began to raise it toward his mouth. Before it got there, the other preacher reached over and slapped it from his hand. It sailed through the air and out the open door where a waiting dog caught it in midair, swiftly gulping it down before the astonished eyes of the entire group.

"So much for predestination," said the Arminian and he began to eat, the argument seemingly ended.

It was just starting. The Calvinist brother rounded up his supporters and they all withdrew their membership from Dewberry Church and started their own. What to name it? Well, they had every right to the name 'Dewberry' since they were all members there. Just call it 'Dewberry #2'. And so it was.

While we are on this subject of intra-church disagreements which become public scandals, usually serving to bring a good laugh in spite of the seriousness of the participants, here's a couple of more examples.

Up in Virginia—I was there on business—they told me the story about a church the locals refer to as 'Half Calvary.' Seems there was a church named Calvary Baptist which had an internal problem and half of them got mad, left and formed a new church, thereafter known as 'Half Calvary.'

Another church nearby had a major split over the fact that a large portion of the congregation wished to purchase a refrigerator. The dissenting half left.

Down in south Georgia, where my old friend Ted used to attend, the church had a proposal come up in a monthly business that they should put the restrooms in the building. Seems like some of the ladies were tired of using the outhouse. The issue caused a major split on the fellowship, culminating in a split in the congregation.

Speaking of outhouses, I was doing mission work down on the Yucatan Peninsula in southeast Mexico among some Indians who had not yet gotten up to that concept. They still used a spot under a shade tree. We built the pastor's family an outhouse. You never saw such proud women.

STORY TWENTY
THE OLD FRIEND

▼

There was this young preacher, whom we'll call Jim. He was in his last year of college and looking for a position. He got a call from a church in a town down on the Mexican border to come preach a couple of Sundays. They were out of a pastor. He went. It was a small, old mining town located in a canyon. The church was out at the edge of town, out of the canyon, the 'new section' of town. From there the view into Mexico was unobstructed.

For a college preacher, it was a real plum position. The church had some of the town's leading citizens, meaning a good income and job security. He could stay on permanent after graduation, might be there several years. Well, a fellow could dream.

The dream came true. After a couple of weeks, the committee asked Jim to be the pastor. He had no trouble accepting. Surely, it was God's will.

The next Sunday, after the morning service, Jim had lunch then took a drive around the area. He parked his car in the old town section and walked around. He couldn't believe his eyes. There, coming down the sidewalk was his old Navy buddy, the man who had been his best friend for three years.

"Gerald," he shouted, running toward the man and hugging him.

"Wow, Jim, what a surprise!"

It had been almost ten years. They had completely lost track of each other. They went to the coffee shop and spent an hour catching up on old times. This was Gerald's hometown. Great! Now Jim would be living here and they'd see each other often.

Gerald was surprised to hear that Jim was a preacher. Jim had become a Christian after he'd gotten discharged. Now Jim insisted that Gerald come to the evening service.

"Come listen to me preach."

"Well, OK, I can do that."

That evening, just at the beginning of the service, Jim was so proud to see his old friend come in the door and sit down near the rear. He couldn't have his old buddy sitting way back there alone. Then came time for announcements and to welcome visitors, Jim went to the stand.

"It's with great pleasure, here on my first Sunday as your pastor, that I can announce to you that I have found here in town the best friend I ever had in my whole life. We've been separated for a few years and what a surprise it was to see him here this afternoon. You just don't know how glad I am to see him again and to introduce him to you here tonight."

He called out Gerald's name asked him to stand. What he did not know was that Gerald needed no introduction anywhere in town. He had for several years had the distinction of being the town drunk.

Jim got that information from a very unhappy deacon board after the service. What a way to start a new career—the pastor who was best friends to the man with the worst reputation in town.

Story Twenty-One
My Friend Pete

▼

I want to introduce you to my friend Pete. I met him in Oklahoma City. I was going to school down at Norman, Oklahoma and went into the city on weekends where I attended the services at the First Baptist Church, a big old downtown church with thousands of members. That's where I met Pete. He was a greeter at the front door. When you entered the church, he made you feel welcome. He was filled with a genuine spirit that made you feel really glad you decided to be there.

Pete was at least old enough to retire, but he worked. There were other contradictions about him, like, he was rich but worked for someone else; he could have afforded a mansion but he lived in an ordinary house. His only luxury, for himself, was a Lincoln Town Car. It was new and nice.

Pete befriended me the first time we met, in spite of the forty plus years difference in our ages. I guess he felt sorry for a kid a long way from home. He invited me to his house for lunch the second Sunday I saw him. That's when

I learned about the car. Seeing it surprised me. He didn't seem like the wealthy type.

After lunch, Pete took me by where he worked. He was a broker at the Cotton Exchange. Along the way, he told me about himself. He had come to the city forty years before with one nickel in his pocket. That was everything he had in the world, except the clothes he wore.

He went to work, saved and invested. He owned two square blocks of prime real estate downtown. He also had a large farm out in the country. The rent on the real estate would have been enough to retire on, if he was so inclined. Pete was different.

Here's an incident about him that I've remembered for a long time. Like I said, Pete was a greeter; had stood by the same door of the church every Sunday morning greeting the arrivals for twenty five years.

One Sunday morning, a man came out the door that Pete had never seen; a man about his own age. Pete greeted him with his usual warm sincerity and said, "I'm awfully glad you came to church today. I do hope you will come back to be with us again next Sunday."

"I probably will, said the other man, "I've been here every Sunday for over twenty years."

"Wait," said Pete, "I've been on this door every Sunday for twenty five years and I've never seen you."

"No wonder to that. I usually go in and out the side door."

Talk about a big church.

STORY TWENTY-TWO
BILL THE BIGOT

▼

My family-Becky and Sallie-and I, lived in San Bruno, California, just south of San Francisco. I was pastor of Immanuel Baptist Church in the town of South San Francisco. There was a couple named Bill and Eva who had been members of the church but had not attended in a long time. I decided it was time to get acquainted with them and get them back to church. One day, I went to visit.

They were nice folks. Came out from Arkansas thirty years before, like lots of folks in the area. Got a good job and just stayed. He had built up enough money to take early retirement from a major manufacturer in town. They owned a nice house. She made a good pot of coffee.

Everything was going along nice and friendly so I decided it was time to get down to the business at hand.

"Bill and Eva, I know you used to attend church at Immanuel and I'd like for you to come on back and joined with us again."

Bill spoke up. After all those years, his Arkansas drawl still came through, "Well, I tell you, preacher, I'm not coming back to that church as long as you got them shines down there."

"Excuse me," I said, question-like.

"You know, shines, spooks, jigs, them niggers."

"You referring to Norm and his family?"

"That's the only shines you got in there."

"I take it you don't care for black people."

"I don't go to church with niggers."

"Bill, you're talking about a man who is a leader in the church and a vice president of Kaiser Corporation."

"We're talking about niggers."

"Bill, you're a bigot, an out and out bigot."

"Call me what you like but I'm not going to church with no shines."

That was that. I prayed for them, like I always prayed for people I visited.

On the way home, I thought about the church. It was my first pastoring position. I'd grown up in the deep South, back during the days of total segregation. We lived by racial separation back then.

I had changed a lot since my boyhood and so had the country. Segregation was no longer the law anywhere in the US, except in the hearts of some people, black and white. But, it was not the rule in my church.

We had white people. We had the Suzakowa family who were of Japanese background. Hank, the father was church treasurer and volunteered to do a ministry to the sick and old folks. Johnny Joel was a Choctaw Indian. He was church organist and a fine musician. I had just baptized a new convert named Hinn who was a native

Hawaiian. Reuben Joseph was a Jew. He had become a Christian but still went to synagogue regularly. The Maldonados were a combination of people descended from Mexicans and Puerto Rican Jews. There were people there who had come from every section of the US, all of them working peacefully and in harmony.

Then, there was Norm and family, the only black family. He was not only a business executive, he was leader of the church's Sunday School and doing a great job. If it came to a choice between his family and having Bill and Eva, I'd rather have him.

But, it was not a matter of choice. Christianity is about changing people's hearts. Bill needed to see that he needed help with his attitude about people. He could at least take a lesson from Granny Brown.

Granny was an old Arkie (person from Arkansas). She had kids as old as Bill. She'd lived lots of her life in segregation and it was still ingrained in her. When she came to church, she made it a point to sit on the other side of the church from Norm. But, she was there. She did not let her upbringing keep her out of her church home.

Overall, I was real happy about the church, happy with the good group of people we had there. I didn't want any disrupting influence but I knew Bill and Eva wouldn't show up till somebody's heart got changed.

I kept going by to see them. Always got the same answer. Bill had the old time argument "you don't want your sister marrying one." In my case he changed it to "daughter."

"How old is your daughter, preacher?" he asked one afternoon.

"She's three, Bill."

"What you going to do when she's about eighteen and comes home one day with a shine boyfriend?" Shine was his favorite word, more so than nigger.

"Well, Bill, that will have to be her decision."

"You won't take it so cool when that day comes, preacher."

Soon after, Bill went to the hospital for major surgery. He had to stay more than a week. I visited him daily. During that time, I noticed a change in Bill's attitude. His stance on blacks really softened. He even decided he'd come to church when he got out of the hospital.

When Bill got home, I visited again. Sunday was coming and I wanted to help him hold on to his decision to come to church. He missed the first Sunday. I kept going back. As the days passed, I noticed something. Bill was slipping back into his old attitude, talking his old talk.

One day, the truth came to me and I just blurted it out as I sat with the two of them, her mother seated in the background, "Bill, I've got it figured out. You're not a bigot. Eva's the bigot."

When I said it, I looked her right in the eye. She was the one who didn't like blacks. Heavens, Bill had worked with them for thirty years at the factory. All those years, Eva had stayed home, keeping house. All those years, her mother had been with her everyday.

I struck a nerve. I struck the truth. The look on Bill's face confirmed it. Eva's look was one of absolute anger. Her crippled old mother even got fiery eyed. Talk about causing an explosion. One thing stopped it from becoming a major disaster. Bill waved his left hand at Eva, the sign for her to shut up, shut up now and stay quiet. Had he not, no telling what she'd have said.

There was no doubt I was right, but Bill was not going to risk problems at home even by coming alone to church. Neither of them ever came.

Bill's words had a certain prophetic fulfillment. Remember what he'd asked me about my daughter bringing home a "shine boyfriend"? Actually, I saw a show on TV last night that brought this whole story to mind. It was about a white father whose daughter was dating a black boy on the sly. Well, my daughter was never one to try such a thing on the sly. She was too open and challenging.

It was about sixteen years after I last saw Bill. We lived in a two story apartment in DeSoto, Texas. Sallie, my daughter, was working at the Burger King in the nearby town of Duncanville. Across the street was an Oldsmobile dealer. At the dealership was a black sales-man named Glenn.

Glenn came to the Burger King on a daily basis. He was thirty, divorced,

looking for female companionship and started hitting on Sallie. Hey, she was a desirable catch; young, pretty, perky, friendly. Glenn came on strong.

His age was a little problem for her but one day she agreed to lunch at Red Lobster. But before they went he had to pick her up at home and meet her parents; her decision. He agreed.

I was upstairs when Glenn came in. Becky greeted him like a member of the family. He sat down in the living room on the couch. We were face to face as I descended the stairs. Sallie was standing by. As I came to the end of the stairs, he stood and she introduced us.

"Daddy, this is Glenn. Glenn, this is my father, Buddy."

I immediately stuck out my hand and shook his cordially. "Glenn, so nice to meet you. Welcome to our home."

There was a little light conversation and they were on their way.

"Have fun," were my last words as they went out the door.

I never saw Glenn again. Maybe it was because he and Sallie didn't really hit it off. Whatever. I do know this. I lived by what I had told Bill sixteen years before. I also know that if I had made a big deal of it, Sallie would have went out with him to spite hell. Sometimes, the easy route is the best route.

STORY TWENTY-THREE
THE BODY OF CHRIST

▼

This is a story about Ernie, a young boy whose parents were Hispanics and lived in the Mexican section near the river in El Paso, Texas. They were strict Catholics. For that reason, everyday after school Ernie had to go by the church on the way home for confession, mass, communion, or classes.

One cold winter day, Ernie went from school to church, shivering all the way. It was the day for afternoon communion. The kids all lined up at the altar and opened their mouths as the priest passed in front of each and place the host on their tongue. For the non-Catholics who might read this the host is a small round wafer representing the body of Jesus in his death. Catholic belief is that when the wafer is blessed by the priest, it actually becomes the body of Jesus.

Ernie was a curious little boy. He had the host placed in his mouth many times and, as instructed, allowed it to melt slowly on his tongue. It is not to be chewed. That would be a desecration. The Bible says that no bone in

Jesus' body was broken. To chew the host would be to break the body of Christ.

Today, Ernie decided it was time to satisfy his curiosity. When the priest put the host on his tongue, Ernie waited till he turned his back, then looked to see that no other kids were looking and took the host from his mouth and put it in his pocket. Swiftly, he was out of the church and across the vacant lot headed toward home.

As soon as he was safely away from the church, and sure that no one else was around, Ernie put his hand into his pocket and pulled out the wafer. He examined it closely. Nothing extraordinary about it that he could see. Just some kind of plain bread looking stuff. It was a little dirty from being in his pocket and getting dirtier from being handled—then it struck him. He was holding in his dirty hand the body of the Lord Jesus Christ and he was getting dirt all over it.

Oh my great gosh, he could be struck dead and go to hell!!! He had to get rid of it. Couldn't eat it-too dirty. Couldn't throw it away. It was holy. What to do? The only thing was to go back to the priest. Ernie hated that thought. The father was strict, hard on boys, very exact in keeping all the rules. But, that was his only choice. He didn't want to die and go to hell.

Slowly, and with much regret over his circumstance, his feet began to take him back in the direction of the church. It was getting closer to being dark. The wind was getting colder. Ernie's heart was a lump of ice. His right hand was in his pocket holding on to the sacred object. He feared it and the possible consequences it carried for his curiosity and guilt.

Reaching the church, he pushed the door open with his left hand, holding on to the host with the right. The priest was near the altar. Ernie slowly approached him. The priest noticed him.

"Yes, Ernie, what do you want?"

Ernie did the only thing he could. His throat was too dry and constricted to speak. He simply held out his right hand with the dirty, shriveled host in it. The priest recognized it immediately.

"What have you done?", he screamed, loudly enough, Ernie was sure, for his mom at home to hear.

"I didn't mean any harm, father. I just wanted to see it."

"You're not supposed to see it. You are surely never to touch it. And look, it's filthy. You have desecrated the body of Christ, the most holy object on Earth. You've got dirt all over it."

Swiftly, but tenderly the priest took the wafer from Ernie's outstretched hand and laid it on the altar. Turning Ernie's body around he spanked him furiously.

"Now, you will do fifty 'Our Fathers' and fifty 'Hail Marys'. Do you
understand?"

"Yes sir, yes father." Ernie was trembling with fear before the red-faced man.

"Never again will you touch the body of the lord. Do you understand?" The question was screamed.

"Yes sir, yes father."

"Get out and pray God lets you live through the night."

Ernie ran from the building and from the fury of the priest. The blast of cold wind outside was a relief. He ran all the way home in the fast approaching darkness.

Years later, when Ernie was a Baptist and I was his pastor, he smiled as he told the story. At the end we both laughed. In the years since, I've thought many times of that cold, frightened little boy running through the slums, his heart filled with fear. I've also thought about Ernie the man who found peace enough to no longer be afraid.

STORY TWENTY-FOUR
MY NEIGHBOR

▼

I moved into this house a little over a year ago, at the end of summer. During the winter, I visited some of the people in the neighborhood. The fact is, I had taken a temporary contract as a salesman with a local cemetery. Hey, a man's got to make a living. About a block from my house, I walked up a driveway past a pickup truck that looked like it was not getting a whole lot of use. By the door was a package just delivered from a medical supply service.

I knocked on the door and waited. Shortly, the door was opened by a man not too many years older than me. He did not look too good physically. The look on his face said things were not good in whatever you want to call his spiritual side.

He was friendly enough. I told him who I was and why I was there. He said he had plenty of burial space, more than he needed since there was nobody but him-no wife. His grown kids could have the extras.

I asked him where his lots were, thinking that if they were where I was working, I could sell him something else, like a grave marker or vault. He told me they were at the buffalo ranch. That sounds strange when you first hear it, but it was the cemetery that was our main competition. It was across the road from a place called The Buffalo Ranch. Seems like everyone I ever talked to remembered the ranch but not the name of the cemetery.

Then, he looked me square in the eye with the saddest look on his face.

"I'll be using mine soon," he said softly. Tears came into his eyes and his face got darker.

"Goodness, brother, I'm sorry to hear that," I told him.

"Oh, it's OK, has to be. It's a fact. I've got cancer. I really don't mind dying. I

just hate going through this. It's too much pain; too much problem. Of course, I'd really rather not die just yet but I'm not worried about being dead. I'm a Christian and got eternity settled a long time ago."

He mentioned a Baptist church in a nearby town. He'd been a member there

for years. The pastor would do his service. Fact is, the church had a cemetery. Maybe he'd get buried there and leave all the lots by the buffalo ranch to his kids.

He faced it all in a matter of fact fashion. Yet there was a sadness to it. The gray in his face wasn't just his disposition. A lot of it was the effect of the disease. I've seen lots of them go with cancer. None looked good, and they all felt even worse. Most times, it has been a blessing to see them dead.

We talked a little about his life. Then, there on his porch I prayed for him. By then he was tired and needed to get back to his chair. We said goodbye. I was saddened by his problem but my own joy in life was heightened by knowing how healthy I was.

I go walking most days. A couple of days ago, I was walking by his house and noticed the old pickup was in the corner of the backyard. In the front yard was one of those big commercial style dumpsters that people get when they are going to have a lot to throw away, like cleaning out an old house or remodeling one.

It brought a mixture of feelings. The old fellow is buried someplace, either out

by the buffalo ranch or in the churchyard. That means his cancer pain has ended. He's no longer suffering physically or just sitting around feeling weak. On the other hand, the life he had loved is ended, never another moment to enjoy any part of it.

When I see the evidence of his mortality of course, I'm reminded of my own. I guess I don't mind dying. I'd just like to be healthy till my day comes. That's why I'm

out there walking most days.

Story Twenty-Five
Oops, My Mistake

▼

Wayne Metcalfe loved two things in this life. He loved to preach and he loved to fish. This is a short, short story about two incidents in his life—one about preaching; one about fishing.

One Sunday morning Wayne was up preaching. You have to remember that, having a great love for preaching, Wayne was a very intense preacher; extremely serious. He wanted his congregation's mood to be serious right along with him. He was also, like many preachers quite loud in his presentation. So, here he was, loud and serious.

Wayne was preaching about the passage in the book of Genesis that tells the story of Abram and Lot separating from each other. He came to the part where he was supposed to say, "And Lot went out on the plains and pitched his tent." His tongue apparently didn't understand the message from his brain. What came out of his mouth was, "And Lot went out on the plains and pinched his tit."

As soon as the sentence was finished, Wayne realized what he had said. By then, the entire congregation was in laughter. No need trying to finish that one. He'd never get their attention back.

The second half of this story is the fishing incident. There was a canal that ran near the town, a big wide canal. People went out there to fish. One day the authorities began letting a lot of water into the canal from a lake upstream. This meant a lot more fish than usual. For days, half the town was on the canal banks fishing. At the first opportunity, Wayne was right there in the middle.

Now, you also have to remember that whatever Wayne did, he was the absolute authority on the subject. So, there he was fishing and he got to watching a young woman beside him, seeing her method of fishing. She was obviously making some mistakes in technique that he did not approve of. After a little while, he could stand it no longer.

"Look, lady, I've been watching you and I want to tell you that you are doing that all wrong."

"Oh, yeah," she said, "I'm catching twice as many fish as you are."

His face was red. She was right. He kept quiet the rest of the day.

STORY TWENTY-SIX
MARVIN

▼

Marvin was a different sort of human and a man of many talents. He was a member of the church and a good friend. Let me give you an example of what I mean by 'different sort of human.' Marvin decided one day that he wanted to learn to play the piano. He had no previous experience, no lessons, nothing—just an ambition. How was he going to learn? He was going to teach himself. If he was going to play a piano, it was going to be the best. He went out and purchased a new grand piano. He did nothing halfway when it came to things he could buy. Did he ever learn to use that piano as a musical instrument? No. His wife got it in the divorce soon after he bought it.

But, before the divorce, they had both been regular in church attendance and seemed to have a good relationship. Another example of 'don't let appearances fool you.' Part of their good public image was the fact that he took her out to eat at least weekly and always took her someplace nice.

One Friday evening, here's the Mr. and Mrs. in the town's most expensive, upscale restaurant having steaks. In the middle of the meal, Marvin heard the man in the next booth coughing as if in agony. He was in agony. A piece of steak had lodged in his throat. He was choking and on the verge of dying.

As soon as he realized what was happening, Marvin jumped up from his seat, picked the man up, did the Heimlich maneuver, dislodged the offending piece of meat and saved the man's life.

"Thanks," the man said, "I appreciate that."

"No problem," said Marvin, "Glad I could help."

They both sat back down, back to back. As they meal progressed and the other fellow got a couple of drinks down, he got louder and louder. His language got more and more profane. This offended Marvin because he knew it offended his wife. He thought she shouldn't have to be exposed to such a lack of respect. He decided to speak to the fellow, taking a rather inoffensive approach.

He said to the man, "Look, I was just wondering, would you mind holding down on the cursing, please? It bothers my wife to have to hear it."

Well, if she had been offended up to that point, she sure got offended now. The man jumped up from his seat and cursed them both, loud and long. He even offered to meet Marvin in the parking lot and do bad things to certain parts of his anatomy, then use those parts to clean up the lot.

Marvin was trying to be a good Christian and be decent in front of his wife. I have a feeling that despite his Christian feelings, if his wife hadn't been there, Marvin would have met the man in the parking lot and left him the worse for the encounter. As it was, he simply excused himself, got his wife by the hand and left.

On Sunday when we talked about it, he was having a hard time understanding why someone whose life he'd just saved would be so mean. I really wished that I had an answer.

But, the thing about Marvin that really stands out in my mind came later. A single man, Brian, moved into town and took up residence in the Savoy, a hotel where singles could live cheap and pay weekly. I ran across Brian and invited him to church. He came, and he came again. We had services Sunday morning, Sunday evening and Wednesday night. Brian was at every service, every week. This went on for about four weeks. One Wednesday, when the service was ended, Brian came to talk to me at the front of the church.

"Buddy, there are some things about your church that need to be changed."

"What are you talking about?" I asked.

He began to tell me how he wanted things done in the church. He got about two paragraphs into his spiel and I stopped him.

"Hold there, fellow. Let me explain something to you. I make the decisions here. I decide how this church will be operated and what our policies will be. Anything I can't decide, the congregation decides democratically. We don't need your help. Besides, what you are saying is contrary to local belief."

He got angry and he got loud. I had greatly offended him.

"You are wrong to oppose me. God sent me here to help you. You are refusing God's demands."

"I'll risk that," I said to him, too loudly.

By now he was headed to the door, still speaking loudly. He passed Marvin on the way out.

Early the next morning, Marvin went to the hotel and right to Brian's room. He knocked. Brian let him in.

"Come on in. I'm getting ready to go to work."

"No, you're not."

"What do you mean?"

"You're leaving town. Pack your bag."

"But, I have no intention of leaving."

"You do now. Pack up."

Brian did as he was told. Marvin had enough interruptions to peace in his personal life; he didn't want any at church. He put Brian in the car and drove him over to the interstate. They stopped at a truck stop.

"OK, Brian, you can get yourself a ride to somewhere from this place. Just remember this, don't ever come back. You've had your last shot at talking to my friend the pastor that way."

Brian took it all seriously. We never heard from him again. Thanks again, Marvin.

STORY TWENTY-SEVEN
MONEY FOR THE FUNERAL

▼

Bill had been sick for a long time, sick enough that the company he used to work for had put him on retirement disability. He spent the last few years of his life as what he liked to call a house husband. Since he could not work, his wife got a job. He stayed home and did the housework.

Bill also did a lot of studying and praying. He had a big house and there was enough room in it for him to have an office. In that office he had his library, most all Christian books, and a desk where he sat to read. To sit at the desk, he had a big, wooden office chair. When he prayed, which was often, he got on his knees and put his head in the chair. He looked at God as his father. When he prayed with his head in the chair, it made him feel like his head was in his daddy's lap.

Bill had a son named Billy. One night, Billy came home late. There was Bill in his office.

"Billy, did you see anybody hanging around the front of the house when you came in?"

"No, Dad, nobody."

"I think somebody's out there."

"I didn't see them. "

"Somebody's here looking for me."

"Goodnight, Dad."

A little while later, another son, Matthew, came in.

"Matt, did you see anyone hanging around the front door?"

"No sir, nobody."

"Somebody's out there. I just know there is. They're here looking for me."

"I didn't see them. Goodnight."

A little while later, Billy got worried about his dad. He got out of bed and went down the hall to the office. There was Bill on his knees with his head in his chair. Something looked wrong.

Billy touched Bill's shoulder, "Dad."

Nothing. Then Billy realized the truth. His father was dead. Then an awesome thought struck him. The 'someone' hanging around the door—Bill was hearing someone from Heaven come to get him. Billy picked up the phone on the desk and dialed Neal's number. Neal was his dad's dearest friend.

"Neal, sorry to bother you so late. Come on over. Daddy's dead."

By the time Neal got there, Billy had Bill's body stretched out on the floor.

"My God, look at that smile," Neal said.

"Yeah, I noticed," Billy replied.

Bill lay dead with the happiest look they'd ever seen on his face, with a huge smile.

"Unbelievable, isn't it?"

"I never saw anything like it. He sure was happy to go."

"I guess he recognized whoever came to get him. He was expecting them."

After the funeral, Billy and his mom discussed family financial matters.

"Your dad kept up his GI insurance. There will be ten thousand dollars. Of course, I'll have to pay for the funeral out of that. It'll take about ninety days to get that. I'm not sure the funeral director wants to wait that long."

"And, that's all you've got?"

"That and what's in the checking account."

"The funeral director will have to wait."

After his mom went to the kitchen, Billy sat in his dad's chair thinking. He began to look at the books on the shelf.

"Say, what is that one doing there?" he said.

There was one book that did not belong. It was the wrong theology.

"He wouldn't read that book, anything like it or anything by that author. Why's he got that book?"

He stood up and took the book from the shelf. He opened it and got a surprise. The inside of the book had been hollowed out. There in the open space was money; lots of money.

"Mom, come here."

They counted the money. It was, to the dollar, exactly the amount owed to the funeral director.

"Billy, it's what we need to pay for the funeral."

"You'll get to keep the insurance."

"Where do you reckon this came from?"

"Dad told me one day he was saving a little out of each retirement check to get you new living room furniture."

"I'm so glad he did. Praise the Lord."

Afterword…In the past few years, I have known two other people whose family found stashes of money following the funeral. Both were women. The first, Geneva, was past eighty and living on a small social security check. After she died, her family found enough ten and twenty dollar bills scattered in the books on her shelf to make up over twenty two hundred dollars. She had once mentioned to someone about having some cash savings in case the banks went broke like back in the depression.

The other was an old lady who lived in some apartments owned by the church she attended. After the funeral, her niece, Jayme, and her cousin went down and cleaned out the apartment. The old lady had lots of literature, including books, brochures and tracts about the church. The two cousins spent an hour carting it all to the dumpster behind the building. They made the last load just as it was getting dark outside. As they were going back to the apartment, the lady across the hall, stuck her head out her door and spoke.

"Did y'all get the money from the books?"

"What money?" Jayme asked.

"She kept all her savings between the pages of them books."

So, in a few minutes, there were the cousins, in the dumpster, using a flashlight, flipping through the pages of every book. It took over an hour. They found a little more than the funeral bill.

Story Twenty-Eight
Left Behind

▼

Life goes on—sometimes good, sometimes great, sometimes bad, sometimes terrible. This story is actually two stories, the stories of two women. Life got terrible.

The first is a woman named Pat. Pat was a wife and a mother. She had a husband and a baby boy. One day she made up her mind she just couldn't be with her husband anymore. They got divorced. She got the baby.

A few years later Pat met and married another man. It wasn't long before she had more kids, four more. The new husband worked. Pat stayed home and cared for the kids.

One day Pat got really sick. She went to the doctor. He sent her for tests. The tests results were bad. The doctor gave the husband the bad news.

"Pat's going to die. She has terminal cancer. It will be a few months. There's nothing we can do."

The husband did something, something quite unexpected. He left. He left Pat terminally ill with four kids to take care.

No, that story does not have a happy ending, unless you count the fact that Pat was a Christian and went to Heaven. She needed it. Her last few months on Earth were Hell.

The other lady was younger, living with her first husband. They had one kid, a little girl. One day she brought her husband the same bad news; cancer, terminal. He walked out on her and the child.

This story ends differently from the last. When this young lady realized what had happened to her, she packed her clothes. She took the baby to her mother's house one afternoon.

"Take care of my baby," she said, "I'm going to New York. I'm not going to die till I've had a chance to live a little."

They never heard from her again.

Story Twenty-Nine
First Funeral

───────▼───────

Every pastor has their 'first' of everything. Some you remember; some you forget. I very distinctly remember my first funeral. I was in seminary and pastoring my first church. I was fortunate to have a full-time church not far from the school.

I had not been there long when I got a call to do a funeral. This was to be the first of many, but that day it was the first and it had several things that kind of put pressure on it. To begin, the family were not members of the church, or any church. Second, the deceased was a nine year old girl. Her name was Caroline. Then, there was the fact that the parents were divorced. The little girl had lived with her mother, Lenore, and a very fine step-father, Stacey. The father, well, that's a different matter.

Let me give it to you in the lady's words, "Pastor, my first husband had a difficult childhood. He was raised by his mother. They were poor-no, poverty stricken. He grew up having nothing. When he grew up, he got a good job and began to really make something of himself.

"After we married he started collecting things. It became a fetish with him. He just couldn't own enough things. We bought this house. As you can see, it's big. He kept buying things. A space as big as this house began to get full."

It was a large house, three floors including the full basement. Each floor was about a thousand square feet. It was tastefully decorated.

"The decoration you see is what I've done since remarrying. Let us show you the basement."

We went downstairs. It was one huge room, with the stairs entering at one end. It was full. The laundry facility was at one side. There was a tiny path from it to the stair. There were tiny little paths here and there through the collection. It was unimaginable, all the things that were there—a collection of Popular Mechanics magazine, complete back to 1910, hunting rifles, old, old Lionel train sets, books by the hundreds; it went on and on. In the corner was a mint condition 1955 Chevrolet Nomad station wagon, all shiny and bright except for the dust that had collected on it. It was unbelievable.

Back upstairs, I had to ask, "What happened to him?"

"One day he just left. He took nothing with him except his car, an old Ford. I haven't seen him since. We heard that he had eventually lost his job. The last we heard, he was parking his car on the street at night and sleeping in it. That was two years ago. When I figured out I'd been abandoned, I filed for divorce. Later, I met Stacey and we married. He was a wonderful father to Caroline. They loved each other."

"If you don't mind me asking," I said, "Why do you still have your house cluttered with all that stuff your ex-husband left here? By the way, what was his name?"

"His name was Travis. We have just kept it thinking maybe someday he'd come around and want it. It was his security blanket. Someday, we thought, he may want it again. We have about decided it's been too long. We're going to begin to dispose of it."

"Let's talk about the funeral arrangements."

"Caroline's body will be cremated. That will probably be going on about the same time we are holding her service. All we want to do is hold a memorial service. It will be day after tomorrow at two o'clock at the funeral home."

"How do you want the service conducted?"

"There will be an organist playing and you will speak. That's all."

We talked then for a while about Caroline. I had already decided that when I started doing funerals, they would be personal. That's something I observe to this day, even after an unknown number of funerals.

At two o'clock on the appointed day, we were gathered in the funeral home chapel. The area where body would normally have been was filled with flowers. The room was filled with relatives, friends, co-workers and even children who were friends of the deceased child. The mom and stepdad were on the first row to my left as I stood in the midst of the bank of flowers.

To this day, I still remember the idea that was basic to the message: Death is the great separator.

About halfway through the message, there was noise in the entry area, which was to the left side of the auditorium. The doors were about halfway down the wall. As the noise increased, the doors opened and in came a man. He was filthy, in ragged clothes, needed a shave and haircut. He looked a little lost.

I stopped speaking. Stacey and Lenore turned to see what was going on. She turned back to me and said just above a whisper, "It's Travis."

Travis, Caroline's long-lost father, obviously a little drunk, started into the room. My first thought was, 'What's about to happen?' I didn't have long to wait to find out. Stacey got up and went to him.

"Come on, Travis," he said, "Come sit with us."

He placed the disheveled man between himself and Lenore. She moved over just a bit to give him room. Then, Lenore took one of his shaking hands and held it. Stacey put his arms around the man's shoulders. It was a reunion of sorts. To me it was lovely, as I continued to speak, to see those two wonderful people welcome Travis into the service and into their hearts. They seemed to understand his need. It was the same one they had. They simply shared their comfort with him.

After the funeral service, Travis disappeared again. Lenore and Stacey heard no more from him. They finally sold his collection just to clear out their house.

STORY THIRTY
NAMING NAMES

▼

A little over thirty years ago, my wife and I were living in Griffin, Georgia. This was in the late sixties. Overall segregation between blacks and whites was still the rule in most of the South. That's what makes the basic elements of this story unusual. It's not a long story, but there's a lesson to be learned.

There was this white man. To save him any further embarrassment, we'll make him up a name. Call him Howard Adams. Howard had a grocery store. You have to remember that in those days Griffin was still a small town and was mostly served by independent grocers. The chain stores hadn't got there yet in force.

Howard's grocery had a lot of black customers, mainly because they could get credit there. This made Howard rather well known in the black section, which was over on the east side of town.

One day Howard got an idea. He figured out a new way to make money from the black folks in town. He'd become an evangelist. He got a tent, some chairs and a piano. He owned some land over in the black section. He set his tent up on his land and began advertising. There would be a meeting every Thursday night from seven-thirty till whenever. Admission was free but an offering would be taken.

Opening night the tent was full. They had about an hour of singing and testifying. Then Howard got up an delivered a stomp-down good sermon with lots of shouting, a little bit of scripture and plenty of amens. It was hugely successful. The offering was overflowing. A few folks even got saved. Everyone left looking forward to being back the next week.

Few new ventures in Griffin had ever been so initially well received, especially when you consider that it was still the era of segregation and this was a white man in the black neighborhood.

It went on week by week for over a year. Howard was well-known to everyone who lived in the section. It was also helping his grocery business, which he didn't mind at all. His income there was increasing and the revival offerings were rolling in.

Then came the night Howard made his mistake. It was discussed in coffee shops around town afterward. Most folks thought he just got overconfident. Exactly what happened was this. Howard decided it was time to call out some specific sins that were being committed right there in the neighborhood. He even began to talk about the sin of adultery. Then he began to name names. He called out the names of husbands whose wives were present. Most of the folks whose names he called were in the service. Howard called on them to come to the altar and pray and repent.

Howard embarrassed a lot of people that night. He made a lot of people angry. It was so bad, as a matter of fact, that the next day, discretion being the better part of valor, Howard took the tent down and got out of the revival business. As they say in Baptist circles, Howard apparently found himself out ahead of where God was leading.

Story Thirty-One
Horn Tooting

▼

The time was the early nineteen thirties. Franklin Roosevelt was president. The country was in the depths of The Great Depression. Howard Giddens, who would later be pastor of the First Baptist Church of Athens, Georgia, was a student at Southern Baptist Seminary in Louisville, Kentucky.

It was summertime. Howard was single and fairly poor and needed a way to spend the evening that would be inexpensive. He did own a car. That was fortunate, because he heard about a Pentecostal revival meeting in a town a few miles away. He drove over.

There was the usual forty-five minutes at the beginning of the service filled with singing, announcements, offering taking and the introduction of the visiting evangelist. From the moment the preacher got into the pulpit, it was evident that here was a charismatic man. Howard, years later, could still tell how the man had a great ability to gain and hold an audience.

Just a few minutes into the sermon, the preacher announced his text.

"Tonight I'll be preaching from just one verse of scripture. It's short. No need to look it up in your Bibles. I'll just quote it for you. I'll be speaking from Deuteronomy 55:55, where it says 'He that tooteth not his own horn shall remain forever in a state of untootedness'."

From there, the preacher took off on a fiery, loud, attention-holding sermon that lasted for nearly an hour. Giddens was amazed. Finally, it came time for the invitation to come to the altar to get saved. A dozen people went forward, kneeling there at the rail and being prayed over and counseled.

It was without doubt one of the greatest nights of revival in the history of the church. It was a night for a young Baptist seminary student to remember. What he remembered most, years later when he told me the story was the fact that he must have been the only person in the church that night, except maybe the evangelist, who was aware of the fact that the book of Deuteronomy only has thirty-four chapters.

One more thing I'd like to tell you about Howard Giddens. He was the pastor at First Baptist Church in Athens during the time of desegregation. It was when the first black students were admitted to the University of Georgia, which was located just down the street from the church.

One day, sitting in his office, I asked him how he was handling the fact that black students wanted to come to his church which, like every other white church in the area, was adamant about segregation.

"Simple, I just tell the people that these are foreign exchange students from Africa. No trouble whatever."

Sometimes there are situations where ingenuity is better than truth.

STORY THIRTY-TWO
ASK THEM TO PRAY FOR ME

▼

Woody Lewis was a hardworking man. He had no choice. He had a wife and family to support. He was also a full-time student at Southwestern Baptist Seminary. His hard work wasn't just on the job making money. It was in the class and in his study working toward his degree.

None of the jobs working for the seminary or at businesses near the seminary paid anywhere near what Woody needed in order to take care of his needs. He was, therefore, self-employed as a paint contractor. He could just make everything work out if he worked at painting everyday.

That's why the accident was such a problem. The accident occurred one day when Woody was high up on a ladder painting the outside of a house. Somehow he slipped. He fell to the ground. He broke his foot. No, he smashed his foot. Here's how bad it was. The attending doctor told him it was so badly broken that it would be six weeks before they could get all the bones set. Then, there would be the healing time after that. Woody was going to be laid up for a while.

Did I mention that his wife didn't work? She had four kids at home. How could she be out looking for a job? She was full-time employed without leaving the house. That means with Woody laid up there was no income whatever. The Lewis family had a problem.

A couple of days after the accident, I was visiting Woody. We'd known each other out in Arizona before we both moved to Texas. He told me what the doctor had told him. We also discussed his strained financial affairs, like, there was no money for groceries since he didn't finish that job.

Just before I left, I mentioned where my family and I were spending the evening.

"Woody, you've heard of the Beverly Hills Baptist Church in Dallas?"

"Yeah, they're that Baptist group that became charismatic, right?"

"Right. We're going over there tonight to attend their Wednesday night prayer service."

"Ask them to pray for me, will you?"

"Sure, be glad to."

What we had heard about Beverly Hills Baptist was just that they had become charismatic in practice and an old church that had been practically dead was now bursting at the seams with people. For their Sunday services, they were renting a local auditorium. The Wednesday night service was still being held in the church building.

If you've ever been to the average church's midweek service, you know that, first of all, the building will be what one man described as 'comfortably full', which is to say, so few people are present that everyone present has room to lay down. Considering how interesting some of those services are, most of those people lying down would be sound asleep.

Truthfully, we had no idea what to expect crowd-wise at the church, but I figured that if they couldn't get their Sunday crowd, morning or night, into the building, we best get there early. Good thinking. Thirty minutes before the appointed time, the parking lot was full and the building was getting crowded.

By the time the singing started, every seat was full, there were people sitting in the window sills, the aisles were full, and there were children sitting on the floor around the pulpit stand. There was no place left to sit or stand. It's a good thing the fire marshall didn't come in.

The service was lively and happy. Everyone was lively and happy. There was no hype, no feeling of force or push. It was all natural and just flowed like a smooth stream. It was the most different Baptist service I'd ever attended. The singing was fantastic. No one could have slept in all that noise.

The message was a testimony from the pastor. More on that later. When it was over, the pastor gave an altar call; 'come for whatever reason you need prayer.' I walked to the front. There was a young minister who served on the staff.

He put out his hand and said, "Hello, My name is Larry. How may I help you?"

"My name's Buddy. I have a friend named Woody. He broke his leg. He can't afford to be off work. There's no income for his family if he doesn't work."

"Then, let's pray for God to heal him."

Larry prayed a very simple prayer asking God to heal Woody. I thanked him and returned to my seat.

The next Sunday night, my family and I went to the evening service at the rented auditorium. It held a lot more people than the church. It was packed.

When the sermon was over and the pastor gave the altar call, I walked to the front. Larry was there.

"Hello, I'm Buddy. We prayed to together Wednesday night for my friend Woody."

"I remember. How is he?"

"He's totally healed and back on the job. I just came to thank you."

"Let's pray together and thank God."

God, in answer to believing prayer, had turned a three month healing period into three days. Hallelujah.

I said before that I'd tell you a little about the pastor's testimony he gave in that Wednesday night service. Here it is.

Beverly Hills was an old church. It was quite prosperous at one time. Through the years, the neighborhood changed. The members moved away and joined other churches. Beverly Hills went down hill in every way.

Rev. Conatser was the pastor. He began to pray quite earnestly about the situation of the church. One day a letter came in the mail from India. The pastor knew no one in India. The letter was an invitation for him to come to India to preach evangelistic services. Quite an order for a man whose church was dying.

To begin, he had no money to go to India. Like preachers are prone to do, he checked the cost. Twenty-seven hundred dollars. That killed the possibility. The next

Sunday, a church member came up and handed him a check, just said God laid it on his heart. In two weeks, without asking, people had voluntarily given him all the money needed for the trip. He decided to go.

When Rev. Conatser got off the plane in India, the pastor who had written to him met him. After the introductions, the pastor said to the host, "How did you get my name and address?"

"God gave it to me in a dream."

"Oh."

They got into a Jeep and rode six hundred miles. Surely after that ride there would be a day two to rest. No. Services were scheduled for that night.

Hundreds—no—thousands were present. It was the greatest service the American had ever been in, by far the greatest. When it was over, his only thought was, 'Now I can go to bed.'

But, no one left.

Conatser asked his host, "Why are they still here?"

"They're waiting for you to have the healing service."

"The what?"

After all, he was a good Baptist and everybody knows Baptist do not hold healing services. Oh well, he was long way from home No one would ever know. It's a good thing God wasn't depending on Rev. Conatser's faith to do His work. A couple of hundred folks got healed.

When the preacher got home, he was changed. Better yet, he could be described as a new man. Soon, the old church was as I told you earlier. Hallelujah.

STORY THIRTY-THREE
ATTEMPTING TO OVERCOME

▼

In the story 'The Tragedy Called Life', I mentioned a man named James and promised to tell more about him later. Here it is.

James had been raised by a drunkard father. His mother and dad had been divorced because the mother, Jewel, was a devout Christian who just wouldn't put up with her husband's lifestyle. As I mentioned in the previous story, the father died as a result of his drunkenness. I did the funeral. James had followed his father's footsteps in alcohol usage. He was overcome by the habit.

Before the father's death, I had been by the house where he and James lived with several of their alcoholic friends and attempted to minister to them all. After the father's death, one morning James and two of his friends came to my house to talk. It was a lovely California day. We sat in the yard under the tree.

James told me his story. It was sad. He'd started drinking young, when the family lived back in Oklahoma. When they moved to the California oilfields, he'd began working regular and drinking daily. Now, he'd seen his father die.

"Preacher, I don't want to end up that way. Maybe God can help me. Do you think so?"

"Well, James, I know God cares about your situation. Why don't we pray and ask him? You just bow your head and tell God what's on your heart and ask for his help."

"I will. OK, you guys, put out them cigarettes. We're going to pray."

Pray James did. He opened up his heart to God, explained his situation and asked for help. Following his prayer, I prayed for him and his companions. They all left feeling happier.

I didn't see James anymore. About a month later, Jewel got worried about him since she hadn't heard from him. She went to his favorite drinking spot, the 332 Club and stood outside the door. She was not about to enter that den of iniquity. A man came by headed inside.

"Excuse me," Jewel said to him, "Do you know James Ingram?"

"Yes, ma'am, I do."

"If he's inside will you tell him his mother is out here to see him?"

"Sure I will."

In a few minutes, James came out. He was drunk. Jewel talked to him briefly then went home, crying as she usually did over him.

The next Friday night, James got arrested for public drunkenness. He spent the night in jail. On Saturday morning, he woke up long enough to eat breakfast then went back to sleep. When lunch came the other prisoner in the cell spoke to the guard.

"That other fellow over there hasn't moved since breakfast time."

The guard came into the cell and took a look at James. "He's dead."

The coroner said it was cirrhosis of the liver due to excessive alcohol usage. James had ended up like his father.

The funeral was graveside only. A few of James' friends and co-workers were there along with his family-Jewel, two brothers, the brothers wives. The casket sat open on top of the grave. James' face was more peaceful than anyone could remember.

For the sake of the family, I tried to be comforting but spoke briefly. After that, those assembled passed by the grave to pay their final respects. I stood at the foot of the grave speaking to each as they passed. Jewel waited till all the others were gone. Then she got up from her chair and walked to the casket.

What you have to know here is that Jewel was an old-time Bible-believing Baptist. Whatever the Bible said and the preacher preached was gospel truth to her. In Jewel's mind, there was no doubt that James had died a lost sinner and was gone to Hell. She was heartbroken.

Tears streamed down Jewel's face as she stood by the casket and reached over to touch her son's face for the last time. I was the only one who heard her last words to him and it broke my heart.

"Goodbye forever, son," she said and turned her back walking slowly away.

As I write this story, Jewel herself is now dead, gone on to a Heavenly reward. I have to wonder, is there any chance that for some reason, unknown to us, she might possibly have met her son on the other side. If she did, it sure would have made her happy.

As part of this chapter, I want to tell you two more stories about alcoholic men I have dealt with, men who were attempting to overcome the problem.

The next fellow was a man named Mac. He had worked for Mobil Oil for over thirty years. He was just an oilfield hand but he had seniority and did a good job. The bosses cared about him. Mac did have a really bad drinking problem. He drank every day, sometimes on the job, always as soon as he got off the job.

One of Mac's supervisors was a member where I was pastor. He got Mac and I together. I met with Mac on a regular basis trying to help him. I even drove him to the AA meetings and sat with him as the people there tried to help him. Nothing worked.

Finally, his boss worked out a deal. There was a clinic in Santa Barbara that specialized in curing alcoholics. The company would send Mac there. The medical insurance would pay the thirty thousand dollar fee. The company would pay his salary all the time he was gone.

Mac left joyfully. He was going to come home cured. He was dry for thirty days. They doctors pronounced him cured and dismissed him. On the way home, Mac stopped at a bar and got drunk.

The next week, I asked him what happened.

"You know they give you them pills that are supposed to make you sick if you have a drink. I just thought I'd test them out."

The company put him on early retirement.

The third man in this trilogy, I met while I was living in Mesa, Arizona. I was the pastor of East Mesa Baptist Church, a small church out between Mesa and Apache Junction. Becky, my wife, was driving in to Phoenix five days a week to go to Grand Canyon College. My old friend Steve (See the story 'Steve') was driving out from Phoenix every Sunday to do the music for me.

For several years, I had a weakness for tent meetings. I'd go to them just for entertainment. I also loved any kind of revival meeting. One day I read about a tent revival being held out at Apache Junction. That night I was there sitting on the back row of the small tent.

The evangelist was a Pentecostal preacher. The meeting was good. When it came time for the altar call, a man got up down front and went to ask the preacher for prayer. The preacher stopped the musicians and addressed the small audience.

"Brothers and sisters, this man whom you see standing before you has come confessing his need and asking for prayer. He's an alcoholic and he's asking for God to heal him. Come and join me in prayer."

Several men and women gathered around and laid hands over the alcoholic. The praying went on loud and long. Finally, the evangelist pronounced him cured 'in the mighty name of Jesus.'

When the benediction was said, I waited in my chair beside the aisle. As the man came out I stopped him and said, "Mister, do you truly feel like you got healed?"

"Truthfully, no."

"Want to talk about it?"

"Yes."

We went to a local cafe. His story went something like this.

"My name is Jerry James. I live over in Mesa. I came to this meeting tonight in pure desperation. I need help. I'm an alcoholic. I do not understand why. I do not like the taste of alcohol, especially beer. Yet, when I drink, I drink beer."

"Tell me about when you drink."

"It's strange. I'll be driving along in my pickup just as sober as can be, thinking nothing about drinking. The next thing I know, it's an hour later, I'm on the other side of town. I don't know how I got there. There'll be an open six pack on the seat beside me with two or three beers gone."

"That's the strangest problem I ever heard."

"Can you help me?"

"Well, I will not pray over you in the form you observed in the tent tonight-not that I think they are wrong. I believe those people to be sincere. You just need something more. I will pray for you and pray with you. I believe God has an answer and will lead you to it. We'll meet on a regular basis for prayer and discussion. Anytime, day or night, you feel you need help, call me."

That was the gist of a thirty minute coffee session. We did meet regularly for prayer. He believed God would lead him to the answer. Then, there came a week when I didn't see Jerry. I began to wonder. One morning he drove into the driveway at my house.

"Buddy, I've got wonderful news."

"Good. Come on in. Tell me about it over coffee."

He had a simple story.

"God has answered our prayers. I was put in contact with a doctor in Mesa. He's a specialist. He did a complete workup. He found out why I have blackouts and wake up drinking."

"And that would be?"

"I'm a hypoglycemic. My body craves sugar. Beer has sugar. When my body needs sugar, I buy beer. He's got me on medication. I'm sick but I'm cured of alcoholism."

Never have I seen anyone so glad to know they were sick. Hallelujah.

STORY THIRTY-FOUR
LET'S GET MARRIED

▼

The last few stories have been serious. Let's lighten up. My dad and I had one thing in common with each other in which we varied from many pastors. We'd do a wedding for just about anybody, anytime, anywhere. I could write a book on nothing but weddings and funerals, funny ones. But, this is a story about Dad.

When he was at his last pastorate before retirement, in the town of LaGrange, Georgia, he lived in a small house out on the highway near the church. One night there came a knock at his door. It was a winter evening and it was dark already.

Dad opened the door. There was a man and woman, people he'd never seen before.

"Can I help you?" he asked.

"The folks down the road said you're the preacher. We have a license. We want to get married."

"Come in."

The couple appeared to be in their thirties. Dad called Mom from the other room. They talked a few minutes and arranged to do the wedding in the living room with Mom as witness.

A few minutes later it was all over. The wedding papers had been signed and placed in the envelope for Dad to mail to the county clerk the next day. Dad had his fifteen dollars in his pocket and the couple got in their car and drove away.

In less than half an hour, there was another knock on the door. It was the man. The woman was waiting in the car.

"Come in," Dad said.

"No, thank you, preacher. This won't take long. Have you still got them wedding papers?"

"Of course. Why?"

"Give them to me. We're going to tear them up. The marriage is off. I couldn't get along with that woman long enough to get out of town."

Dad gave him the envelope. He tore it up, got in the car and drove away, fussing at the woman as they left.

While we're on the subject, I'll throw in one more. My friends Kenny and Joy wanted to get married. This was in Phoenix. The wedding was planned for sundown at Papago Park, a large park on the east side of town.

Besides being in the park, everyone in the wedding party was to be on horseback. As it began, it looked good. I stood on a rock in a flat place at the top of a rise with a hill in the immediate background. Up from the valley came the wedding party, all on horses. The guests were gathered around forming a semicircle with room for the horses to get to me.

In a few minutes, there we all were. I began the vows, speaking loudly and slowly. Suddenly, the party was struck by a big puff of wind. I looked to the west. Coming toward us from the direction of town was the biggest sandstorm I'd ever seen. No time for much ceremony.

I turned back to the bride and groom.

"Kenny do you take Joy to be your wife?"

"I do."

"Joy, do you take Kenny to be your husband?"

"I do."

"Then, you're married. God bless you. Let's get out of here."

And off they galloped to the shelter of the leeward side of the hill.

STORY THIRTY-FIVE
THE MEETING

▼

Ron was a member of a small but elite group in the little town where he lived. That little group of five people controlled all the illegal drugs on the west side of the county. That was a sizable territory with lots of pushers working under them. It was a lucrative territory. Or, as Ron liked to say, "Not bad for a side income to supplement my salary."

The fact was, he did have a job, a nice legal, visible job that made him look nice and legal. The profits from the dope trade were well hidden. No government agency was ever going to follow an income trail to convict him of illegal activities.

One Monday night, the group was holding their weekly meeting. They were at a home belonging to one of them, seated around the dining room table, four men and one woman. The discussion was going along as usual. If you hadn't known what it was about, you might have figured it was a meeting about any legal sales business. There was talk of sales figures, salespeople, territories, volume broken down into different types of products, supply and distribution.

Suddenly, in the middle of talking about gross profits, the one lady present, who was sitting directly across the table from Ron, looked at him and said, "Ron, you need to accept Jesus Christ as your Lord and Savior. There is a necessity for you to become a Christian and do it now."

Ron looked at her like a man who had just been hit in the face with a wet mackerel.

"What are you talking about and why?" he asked.

"I have absolutely no idea. It just came into my head. I don't know where it came from."

They went back to talking about drugs. Soon after, the meeting broke up.

Ron worked a little over a mile out of town, making it about a mile and a half from home. The next morning, he was driving to work as usual. Suddenly, about a half mile from home, the scene changed. All he was seeing was a bright light. The car was still moving, but he was unaware of how. He wasn't even thinking about it. All Ron saw was the light.

In the light, Jesus began to talk to him, "Ron, I want you to believe in me. Let me become your Savior. I want to give you a new life."

Ron was convinced by the voice and the light that he was talking directly to God. He began to talk back.

"Yes, Lord, I do accept you as Lord. I will let you have my life and make me whatever you want me to be."

The overall conversation was a little longer than that but that is essentially the exchange that went on between them. When the conversation ended, the light went away and Ron found himself parked in his spot at work.

"Wow, I'm a Christian now. I've never felt so good."

Not long after that, Ron became a student in the seminary classes I taught and his wife became a teacher in the school at the church I pastored. They were two of the most devoted people I ever met.

STORY THIRTY-SIX
AS I WAS SAYING

▼

Going north out of Sacramento, as you get to the northern edge of the central valley and come to the lower side of the foothills, there's the town of Redding. Just outside Redding, you'll find one of the most picture perfect little church buildings in California. It's a white frame building, with tall old-fashioned windows, located out of town, back up off the road, in a grove of trees—a truly ideal setting, like what you see on postcards. It didn't even have air-conditioning. It wasn't needed. Being located in the foothills under a grove of trees gave the building good temperature control.

The unique location and the nostalgic beauty of the building make it quite popular as a place for weddings, small ones of course. You couldn't get a hundred folks in the auditorium unless a lot of them stood up.

Pastor Ron was having an enjoyable tenure as the leader of this small group of Christians. This meant he also did more than a normal amount of weddings. This is the story of one of those weddings.

It was a beautiful Saturday afternoon in the summertime. A wedding was in progress. The tall windows were all open. These windows were only about two feet wide each. They began eighteen inches off the floor and stood over seven feet high. With a little breeze coming through the grove, it was comfortable. The double doors coming into the church were open as were the two inner doors leading from the small entryway into the main room.

There was a center aisle leading from the doors directly to the pulpit area. The pews on either side were packed with guests. The pulpit stand had been removed from the dais, giving plenty of room for the wedding party to be on a level just above the main floor.

The wedding party was all in place facing the minister with the bride and groom in the center. Pastor Ron was just completing the bride's vow saying "…as your lawfully wedded husband?"

He looked up from his book to the bride for her answer and the bride noticed his face go blank. He was looking between the bride and groom down the center aisle where out of the corner of his eye, he had just caught sight of a cat coming in the front door. The cat wandered casually down the center aisle. Soon, everyone was following Pastor Ron's gaze and seeing the cat. Even the bride and groom turned to see what was going on. The entire crowd seemed mesmerized by the animal.

The cat came down the aisle, up the single step onto the platform, walked around the bride and went over to the groom. She pressed herself against the groom's leg, raising her back and rubbing against his pants. She was making her way around his leg to give herself a good all over rub, when her gaze went to the front door. Everyone followed her gaze.

There in the middle of the doorway, outlined by the incoming afternoon sunshine, was a big dog-no-a huge dog. He got as far as the inner doors and saw the cat. Immediately, he began bounding down the aisle. The cat hesitated briefly then turned and ran to the nearest window, leaping for it from three feet back. She cleared it and was gone.

The dog, toenails clicking on the hardwood floor, raced down the aisle, leaped onto the platform between the bride and the maid of honor. Slipping sideways, he turned and went between the bride and groom and the minister. A few feet away, he took a great leap and sailed through the same window the cat had used.

Not a sound had come from anywhere in the church except those made by the dog's feet. Now, all eyes turned back to Pastor Ron. He looked at the bride and said, "Do you take him as your lawfully wedded husband?"

"Oh, uh, yes, yes, I do."

As is so often the case, the story brings to mind a similar one. This one is about my old friend the late Bill Hintze, former president of Grand College in Phoenix, Arizona. When I met Bill, he was an assistant professor, teaching classes in preaching.

In his preaching classes, Bill taught the value of copious notes. He believed every preacher should go into the pulpit every time with plenty of written material. This story is one he used to illustrate the reason for that idea.

Before coming to the college, Bill had been pastor of a small church. Back then he had always used quite extensive notes in his preaching, almost like a manuscript. One bright spring day, when all the doors and windows in the small auditorium were opened wide, Bill was in the midst of his sermon, as is often expressed 'waxing eloquently'.

In the middle of a point a little boy about six or seven years old, got up from his seat beside his mother, walked out the center aisle to the rear doors and went down the steps. By now, Bills curiosity had reached the point that he stopped talking in mid-sentence.

At the bottom of the steps, the little boy, back to the church, unbuttoned his fly, urinated, buttoned back up, turned around and came back up the steps. No one had seen his actions except the preacher. No one knew why Bill had stopped talking.

As the boy came back down the aisle toward his seat, Bill picked up the sentence exactly at the word he had left off and completed the thought.

"And that, men," he told us, "is one very good reason for using good notes. It covers the unexpected."

STORY THIRTY-SEVEN
THE EVANGELIST

▼

Mr. Kerr was born and raised a Catholic. He married a Catholic lady. They raised their one son Catholic, sending him to Catholic schools and to a prestigious Catholic university. Now, Mr. Kerr was old, sick and dying. He lay on his deathbed in a Catholic hospital being attended by nurses who were all nuns.

His son sat in a chair in the corner of the room. He knew the time of his father's departure was near. He was simply waiting loyally, out of love. The son believed his father to be either asleep or in a coma. The old man hadn't been awake in hours. The doctors and nurses had done their regular checks on him. His breathing was gentle, slow, quiet. There had been no movement of any kind since the son had arrived two hours before.

Into the room came a nun. Back in those days, it was easy to be sure. That was in the times when nuns, even nurse nuns, wore the habits which distinguished them from everyone else. This nun was unusual. She was short, so short that she carried around with her a small wooden step to use to reach the height of the hospital beds. Again, this was in the days when hospital beds were permanently set higher than the ones in today's institutions. The son was sure of one thing. He'd never seen this particular woman in the hospital before. He was surprised to see her now.

This little nurse, about four and a half feet tall, came into the room carrying her wooden step-box, put it down beside the bed, stepped up on it and spoke into the patient's ear.

"Mr. Kerr, have you ever accepted Jesus Christ personally as your lord and savior?"

To the son sitting in the corner, it seemed a strange way to approach a man who had apparently been asleep or in a coma for hours. He was surprised when his father, eyes still closed, spoke a single word in reply.

"No."

"Then, Mr. Kerr, you need to pray right now, ask Jesus to come into your heart as your savior, make you a child of God and cleanse you of your sins."

His eyes still closed, the old man began to speak, "God, I do pray to you now, in the name of Jesus, to forgive me of my sins and cleanse my soul. I now accept Jesus as my savior and ask him to come into my life and give me a place in your kingdom. Thank you. Amen."

The little nurse said no more. She got down off the stool, picked it up and went out the door. Once again Mr. Kerr was silent. The son sat quietly in his chair, watching thinking, amazed at what had just taken place. Two minutes later, Mr. Kerr breathed his last breath.

STORY THIRTY-EIGHT
FAIR PAY

▼

For years the lady had followed the activities of two evangelists and supported both them generously. She believed they were both true men of God and she wanted to help all she could. These men were not rich. They weren't on radio or TV. They simply went from church to church, town to town, preaching the gospel and exhorting sinners to accept Jesus. Through the years, many had. That's what impressed the lady. She believed in that sort of Christian work. She couldn't do it herself, but she was willing to do all she could to support those who did.

Now, the lady had died. Her body had been taken to Sunset Funeral Home where Myron had been given the responsibility of taking care of all the arrangements. Her children told him all her wishes concerning the funeral and asked him to take care of it. They put up plenty of money to see that it was all handled exactly according to her wishes. Myron, being a conscientious man was doing just that.

The deceased had requested that both the evangelists speak at her funeral. She liked them both too much to leave either out. Both of them lived in a town about thirty-five miles away. Myron called them both. Yes, both were available on that day. Yes, both would come.

Came the day of the funeral. One evangelist called the other.

"Listen, brother, there's no need both of us traveling way over there for that funeral. Why don't you just do it alone. You take whatever honorarium there is all for yourself and just express my regrets to the family."

"OK, seem like a good enough plan to me."

So it happened that only one minister showed up for the funeral. He did a bang-up good job. The family was unhappy about the other fellow's 'sudden urgent business' but they were understanding. After all, these men had to go as God led. But, they were happy with the job done by the one who came.

When it was all done, the family was all gone and they were ready to lower the casket into the ground, Myron approached the minister.

"I'm so sorry your friend couldn't get here to help you out. Too bad you had to do it all alone."

"Well, we do what we can, accepting the circumstances as they arise."

Then he told Myron the truth about why he was the only one of the two present.

Myron's reply was, "Well, at least you'll be paid for coming. The lady had specified that each of you should be paid for your time. I was directed to make out duplicate checks for each one of you."

With that, he pulled two envelopes out of his coat pocket. He handed one to the preacher.

"Your friend didn't earn his so only you will be paid."

He tore up the other envelope and put the pieces back into his pocket.

The preacher opened his envelope and looked at the check. Two thousand dollars!! He was sure glad he came. Too bad about his friend.

Story Thirty-Nine
Interpretation

▼

My family and I had just moved to Lancaster, Texas which was to be my headquarters. The first week there, I kept passing an interesting looking church building on the main street. The sign said a woman was pastor and that the church was charismatic. Having just served as a Baptist church for seven years and now being free to attend anywhere when I wasn't preaching, I decided to give this one a try. Curiosity, I guess.

On the following Sunday, we were there. The song service was good. I like lively music, and that certainly was. At the end of the music, when the lady got up to preach, a member of the congregation spoke briefly in tongues. The pastor waited respectfully while he finished.

Then, she continued waiting, feeling that someone would have the interpretation. Suddenly, in my heart, I knew it was me. Although I had previously been in churches where tongues were spoken, this was the first time I had ever felt that I had the answer to the message. Frankly, being a bit shy about being in a new place, I felt that maybe someone among the regulars might also have the interpretation, so I kept quiet.

The pastor waited about a minute, then said, "Someone here has the interpretation."

She waited again briefly. Then, she looked directly at me, pointed her finger at me, and said, "You have it."

Wow, was I ever surprised. Right then I figured that there was a woman who was definitely in touch with God.

Story Forty
To Hell With You

━━━━━━━━━━━▼━━━━━━━━━━━

This story originally appeared in my book 'The Legend Lives On'. I am inserting it here because it is distinctly Christian and it is a real thought provoker.

"You listen to me, old woman. I've had it with you. I've had it with this farm. I'm sick of being poor. I don't intend to be stuck out here in the country outside this hick town any longer. I've had all I intend to take of you and all of it. I'm leaving. There's nothing you or anyone can do to stop me. To hell with you and all of this."

"Don't talk like that, Darlene. Don't talk about Hell. You know it's real. Talking like that could make you end up there."

"The hell you say, Mama. I don't believe that. I don't believe in none of your church stuff. Religion is just a way to keep poor folks happy with being poor. Well, I ain't having nothing else to do with your religion, your church, your preacher—none of it 'cause I'm giving up being poor.

I'm giving up being told how I can live my life. Ain't nobody telling me ever again that I can't smoke, drink or dance if I want to. Not you. Not nobody. You understand?"

Darlene and her mother were having this argument as she packed what few belongings she had into the only suitcase they owned. What she said was true. They always had been poor, even when her father was alive. When he died young of cancer, that left her and Mama to fend for themselves as best they could. Mama thought they were fortunate that the farm was free of any mortgage. At least, they had a place to live. Mama had scratched out the best living for them she could between what she could raise for eating and selling on the farm and a few part-time jobs around the area.

It had been five years that they had lived that way. Darlene was tired of it. She was tired of boring hellfire and brimstone sermons at the church. She was tired of dull people. She was tired of that silly little town. She intended to go someplace exciting—someplace like Birmingham, Montgomery or maybe even New Orleans. Yeah, those kind of places were her style; not this hick town.

Last night she had made a deal with Luther Hendricks. He'd drive her to Birmingham and arrange a place for her to stay and help her get a job. In exchange there were some favors he wanted, some he'd been wanting for a while. Darlene looked forward to spending a few nights paying him off.

Just as Darlene clicked the latches on the old suitcase, she heard a horn honking outside. She picked up the suitcase and went to the front door. She stopped long enough to say, "Don't look for me back, Mama. I ain't coming."

With that she slammed the door and was gone into the night. Mama stood sobbing, tears running down her cheeks. First her husband. Now her only child. Oh Lord, how could she go on?

She found the answer to that question. She went on. Life went on. She was strong. She'd been raised on hard times. Inside she was tough. She also had her faith, her church and her friends. She never missed a church meeting, whether regular services or revivals. She was at all of them, no matter how much effort it took. Every night she read her Bible and prayed. Every night she prayed for Darlene. Every morning before breakfast she prayed in thankfulness to God. Every morning she prayed for Darlene.

When Darlene had left the little Alabama town, World War II was in it's second year. That was March, 1943. Wartime rationing made things a little harder for Mama. Gas and tires for the old car were hard to get. Sugar and meat were rationed. Meat wasn't a problem for her. She raised chickens. They provided meat for her table. The wartime economy also brought a degree of prosperity. That meant higher wages whenever she had a job some-place. She made it through.

She also made her home a haven for traveling ministers. It was her way of thanking the Lord for his kindness to her. Anytime a traveling evangelist was holding meetings locally, he was welcome to stay in her home. There were three bedrooms—Mama's room that she had shared with her husband, the one the preachers used which had always been their guest room, and there was Darlene's room. Mama kept it just like Darlene left it. When she cleaned house, she cleaned that room just as though Darlene were living in it.

In the late summer of 1948, Mama's prayers were answered. One evening there was a knock at the front door. Mama went to answer. There stood Darlene—pale, thin, weak looking, a look on her face that mixed shame and defiance. Mama hugged her.

"Come on in, baby. Welcome home."

"I'm tired, Mama. I want to go to bed."

The next morning, Mama was up early. She warmed up the fried chicken left over from the night before, scrambled some eggs, made a pot of grits and baked a pan of biscuits. She waited patiently. Darlene didn't get up. Mama went to the bedroom door, opened it quietly and looked in. Darlene was still asleep. Mama ate alone.

Finally, at eleven o'clock, Darlene woke up, but she didn't get up. Mama took her a cup of coffee.

That's all she wanted.

"You want to talk about anything, Darlene?"

"You might as well know the truth, Mama. The reason I came back is because I'm sick. I can't work. I'm out of money. The bus ticket home took my last cent. I'm here 'cause I can't be no place else."

"What kind of sick, Darlene?"

"I don't know. I couldn't afford a doctor."

"We'll get Doc Blanchard out here to see you. I'll figure out how to pay him."

"Now, Mama, I want you to know that I haven't changed my mind about anything. I'm not going to church while I'm here. When I get well, I'll leave again."

"I understand. While you're here, you'll get good care."

"Mostly, I just want to be left alone. I'm too sick to be having anybody bother me, including you."

With that she lay down and turned her face to the wall. Mama went to the kitchen, knelt by the table and prayed. She had no telephone so after eating lunch she rode into town and talked to the doctor.

"I'll be by on my way home, Mrs. McCurley. About five fifteen."

He came. He went into Darlene's room and stayed a long time. When he finally emerged, there was a sad look on his face. He sat at the kitchen table, drank coffee and talked.

"She's sick to death, Mrs. McCurley. She won't leave this house alive. Mostly, it's cancer, same as your husband. Her lifestyle has aggravated the problem. She's rundown. No resistance. She has a venereal disease. I'll tell Tom over at the funeral home that you'll be needing him soon."

"Thank you, Doctor. What do I owe you?"

"One more cup of coffee. Nothing else."

The next day, Saturday, Reverend Philmont arrived. The summer revival at the church was scheduled to begin the next day and go on for two weeks. The Reverend would be staying with Mama all that time. He had stayed at the McCurley house before. Mama was glad to see him back. She explained to him about Darlene.

"Yes, I remember from the last time I was here. The Lord has sent her back to you."

"If she must die, I would rather it be here with me."

After supper, Mama went in and asked Darlene if the Reverend could come in and see her.

"No!! No!! you hear me? No. I don't want that Bible-thumper in here trying to get me saved. I ain't repenting of anything. I don't want to be prayed over. Keep him out of here."

Darlene got weaker everyday. When the preacher had been there a week, she went into a coma. Mama called the doctor out on Sunday afternoon.

"She won't be waking up," was his only comment.

Mama looked at her daughter lying in the big old double bed that had belonged to her grandmother. It had a tall headboard made of oak that reached almost to the ceiling. Mama loved that old bed. She loved her daughter even more. She'd got her back, just to lose her again. Thank God, she had her for this short time.

By Tuesday night, Darlene's breathing was so shallow as to be almost unnoticeable. The Reverend insisted that Mama stay home from the service. Regrettably she agreed. She hated missing the service but she couldn't leave Darlene alone.

Rev. Philmont got back at nine-thirty. He and Mama sat in the livingroom discussing the blessings that had been on the evening's service.

"Oh, it's so good to see folks responding to the word of God," Mama said.

"That's true, sister. That's the feelings of my heart."

"I only wish that somehow Darlene could......"

Her words were cut short by a loud scream from Darlene's bedroom. Both of them jumped up and ran to her door. Mama slammed it open. There was Darlene, hands on the headboard, climbing it backward, staring downward, screaming.

"Get those flames away from me!"

"Darlene," Mama cried.

The girl pushed herself further toward the ceiling.

"My feet are on fire. They're burning!" She screamed out the words. Her agony was evident. By now her head touched the ceiling.

"I'm burning. The flames are burning me. My feet are on fire. It's coming up my body.!"

With that, she fell face forward into the bed. Mama and the preacher raced to her side. He reached for her pulse. Nothing. He tried the jugular vein. Nothing.

"She's dead, Mrs. McCurley."

"Preacher, did she go to Hell?"

"I can't offer no comfort, Ma'am. We leave her in God's hands."

A year later Rev. Philmont sat in the kitchen at my father's house and told him that story. I sat in the corner listening. As an eleven year old, I was impressed. Since then, I've had probably a hundred occasions to travel down the highway near where Darlene died. That picture of her on the headboard comes to mind every time. Did she go to Hell? You judge.

As a minister, I have done many funerals. People often ask me about the eternal destiny of someone who has died whose relationship to God was doubtful. I always tell them, "He's in the hands of a fair and just God." Like the final words of Rev. Philmont in the story, I will condemn no dead person.

STORY FORTY-ONE
DESSIE

▼

Dessie and Monty are such a perfect couple. They appear to have been made for each other, one of those couples that you are sure, upon meeting them, that they have had fifty or more happy years together. Actually, Monty's only been bringing joy into Dessie's life for nineteen years. Before that, for Dessie, life was quite different.

Her story begins when she was a young lady and got married. Her husband, Leroy, (made-up name) joined the Navy while they were still newlyweds. He did get home now and then. During that time, he made Dessie the mother of a beautiful baby girl. They named her Peggy.

After his tour in the Navy, Leroy came home where Dessie was living with her parents. He did not seek to become employed. He had made up his mind that Dessie's father could support him. Dessie divorced him and got custody of Peggy.

A few years later, she married another Navy man, this time an officer who was a career man. This man had a position that made him capable of supporting Dessie and

Peggy. He was a commander in the chaplain corps. There was one little problem in this marriage. The husband, Jeremy, (made-up name) had an ex-wife. She was a constant problem. She was calling and coming by. She was threatening. It was an almost daily menace. It was ruining Dessie's life. The real problem was that Jeremy wasn't the one catching all the flak. When the problems with the ex-wife really got bad, Jeremy was out at sea. Dessie took the brunt of it.

During this time, Dessie's father died. That was especially meaningful to her because of the great love she had for him. Their relationship had been something special, the one great stabilizing factor in her life. Now, she felt alone. Somehow, she survived long enough to get Peggy grown and married. Seeing Peggy move all the way across country was a shock that brought an even greater loneliness to Dessie. There she sat alone in California with a husband who was never there and his ex-wife who always was.

The day came when she could take it no more. For several days, she contemplated what seemed to be the best solution. She would simply kill herself. She even figured out how. Not far from her house there was a big tree right beside the road. She would drive her car into the tree.

One morning, Dessie got herself dressed, then sat down and wrote out suicide notes, one to Peggy and one to Jeremy. She got into her new Mercury and started down the road. As she got near where the tree was, she sped up. There was a noise in the back seat and the touch of a hand on her shoulder. She looked into the rearview mirror. Looking back at her was her father! His hand was on her shoulder.

He spoke, "Don't do this. Peggy needs you."

She increased the speed of the car.

Again he spoke, "No. Peggy needs you."

The pressure of his fingers on her shoulder was increased.

She didn't speak back to him, only kept her course in defiance. He kept urging, reminding her of her daughter. Just before hitting the tree, she yielded to the pressure of his urge, slowed the car and changed course back onto the roadway.

Trying to overcome the effect of the problems in her life, Dessie began to see a psychiatrist. Finally, the only reasonable course seemed to be divorce. She walked away from marriage number two. She could support herself. She was employed by civil service. To get away from the scene of the bad marriage, she took a transfer to Arizona.

Peggy was married to a man we'll call Cecil. In 1971, she became the mother of Melissa. It was about that time that her marital problems started. Cecil was turning into a bad personality, one who was hard to live with. Peggy decided that she would leave him. He threatened suicide saying she'd be responsible for his death. She stayed. How many thousand times she must have regretted that decision.

A detailed telling of Dessie's story would be a book, not just a short story. This would be especially true of the events of Peggy's life for the next few years. Most all of those details would be negative. In those years, one very positive thing happened to Dessie. She accepted a transfer to Fort Gordon, a large army installation near Augusta, Georgia. This put her almost two thousand miles closer to Peggy and Melissa. It also brought her romance.

At Ft. Gordon, Dessie met and married Monty, the best male experience of her life, the only really good thing since the passing of her father. The wedding took place in 1981. His support would prove vital to Dessie over the coming years.

In 1991, after thirty-four years of civil service, Dessie retired. She and Monty went on a six week tour of the western US. During that time, being worried about Peggy, Dessie called her every week. Monty and Dessie got home from their trip in August. On September second, Peggy called. She had cancer in both breasts, the lymph nodes and her vascular system.

Dessie drove down to see her in Cocoa Beach. She had to go alone. Cecil wouldn't allow Monty or any other friends to come. Peggy, who liked reading, was only allowed by her husband to read materials about cancer. Monty found a nearby condo where he could stay in order to give Dessie the personal support she would need. It was support that would become vital. The ordeal would last for one long, hard year.

During that year, Monty and Dessie were back and forth between southern Florida and home in Georgia. Peggy was shuttled back and forth between home and a cancer clinic in Tampa. In October, the doctors started chemotherapy. During this time Melissa was attempting to go to college, and getting no help from her father. Quite the opposite. She wasn't even allowed to live at home or see her mother. Cecil was making life hard for everyone. During this time, he got a hip replacement. Dessie took care of him as well as serving as primary care-giver for Peggy. He got OK. Peggy didn't.

In January, she had a double mastectomy. Next came a bone marrow transplant, an extremely painful procedure. In March, Cecil got fired from his job. He didn't tell Peggy. That was when the doctors began radiation treatments. At Easter time, the local Methodist church, expecting Peggy home, dedicated their flowered cross to her. She was too sick to be there. She did get home in May. The entire town where they now lived turned out for her.

At this time, Peggy actually had gotten to feeling stronger. She went back to her job. That only lasted three weeks. Then it was back to Tampa where she was diagnosed with cancer in her lungs, brain and liver. She had real faith in the possibility of recovering. She made plans for it.

Peggy had her forty-seventh birthday on September first. Melissa turned twenty-one on September eighth. On the seventeenth, Dessie got a call. Peggy was dying. She and Monty drove down as quickly as possible. Peggy died at eleven-thirty. Dessie and Monty arrived ten minutes later. Dessie went into the room and held her dead daughter's hand. It was still warm.

During the year of Peggy's ordeal, Dessie had been back and forth several times between home and Florida. She'd stayed as long as two months at the time. Monty, saintly man he is, was always there to support her. She, too, was going through a physical ordeal just trying to find the strength to bear it all.

Once, after a particularly trying time, instead of taking her home when she left Peggy's, Monty had booked a nice, relaxing cruise. That's the kind of fellow he is.

Dessie still makes a strong connection between that year of Peggy's cancer bout and the day in California she almost killed herself, the day her dead father came to her and said, "Don't do this. Peggy needs you." He was certainly correct. Beforehand, she could never have imagined just how correct he would prove to be.

Sitting at Dessie's table, taking notes for this story, I asked her if it was worth living through two bad husbands and one bad son-in-law to get to the point in her life of having Monty. "Definitely," she said, "definitely worth it."

Oh yes, about Melissa. She made it through college. Now she works in administration at Disney World. For her, life is a real-life fantasy.

As this book goes to press, Monty has had a light heart attack. He's OK, though. He was in Bible class this morning. Praise the Lord!!

Story Forty-Two
Butch's Brother

▼

Butch was one of those people who was just a delight to know. He was pleasant, always happy and had a smile every time you met him. He was a hardworking man with a wife and two great kids, a girl and a boy. I liked Butch the first time we met.

Butch had not been raised a Christian. He knew little about it. We met because his wife's grandmother was a member of my church. That led me to meet his mother-in-law, who joined the church, which led me to Butch and his wife. Like I said, Butch didn't know much about church and such stuff, but he soaked it up anxiously. In one way or the other his whole extended family on his wife's side was involved. (His brother-in-law was Randy of the story 'Resurrection.')

After attending a weeknight Bible study, which I was holding at his in-laws house, Butch decided that he needed to become a Christian. I witnessed to him. He prayed and invited Jesus into his life. We scheduled his baptism for the following Sunday night.

On the appointed night, he was there, not just with his wife's family but his own, all of who lived in another town about fifteen miles away. He introduced me to them.

Then he said, "Buddy, this is my brother. He wants to talk to you personally before the service begins.."

"Well, we've got some time. Let's all three step into the church office over here and talk."

In the office, Butch was direct, "Buddy, I told my brother how much of a difference getting saved has already made in my life. He's decided that he wants to be a Christian too."

"Great," I answered and began a brief talk with the brother, Dale, to be sure he understood exactly what we were talking about. Butch had done a good job. Dale had a good understanding. A few minutes later we all knelt on the carpet and Dale asked Jesus into his heart.

When we were seated again, I asked Dale if he thought he understood enough about the commitment he was making to go ahead and be baptized that night along with his brother.

"Yes, yes, most certainly. I'd love it. You know, this all means that I am now unemployed."

I wondered what becoming a Christian had to do with him losing his job.

"Why would you become unemployed because you're a Christian?" I asked.

"Simple, I'm a dope dealer."

"Oh yes. I understand."

Here's another little story that involves Butch. Not too long after he became part of the church, he got laid off his job. It was a political matter, that is, office politics, and there was no doubt he'd get it back. Fact is, he eventually did. Meantime, he had two kids and a wife. No job. No groceries.

About two weeks after Butch got laid off, Paul and I were cutting the weeds that grew along the chain link fence between the parking lot and the road. He was on the roadside. I was in the parking lot. We were both digging along when he looked down and said, "Hey, look at that."

Right by his hoe was a one hundred dollar bill. He picked it up and put it in his pocket. That was the end of it.

The next Monday morning, Butch went out to his mailbox. Inside was a plain envelope. No stamp. No address. Just the word 'Butch.' Surprised and mystified, he opened it. There was a fifty dollar bill. Wow! Groceries.

The next Monday morning, Butch went out to check his mail. Another envelope. Another fifty dollars. More groceries. That week he got his job back. The next Monday, no envelope.

Now, I wonder. Was there any connection between the fence money and the grocery money? Paul never said what happened to the hundred dollars. How do you reckon that money got in that weed patch in the first place? God knows.

STORY FORTY-THREE
ONE MORE WEDDING STORY

▼

As I stated before, I have never had any real personal restrictions about doing weddings. That has led to some unusual ones, like the one on horseback, one in a beautiful grove of tall trees on top of a mountain, a very private wedding with a pregnant bride, and a Christmas morning wedding, among others. That last one only lasted three months. Well, this is the last wedding story in this book. Unless I change my mind, it will be the last story of any kind in this book.

The groom's name was Don. His bride was Linda. He was a good man with a responsible job who was very good at what he did. He had the ability to support her. She was a lovely young lady. They adored each other. They were in love with each other and with life.

They got the wedding all planned and asked me to officiate. I wasn't pastoring at the time. They arranged to use a church near her house. Everything was all set up for a Friday evening. It was springtime in the desert, a lovely time of year.

It was a beautiful little white, frame church, just right for the number of guests that were invited. It was tastefully decorated. Over in the groom's preparation area, Don and his best man were all excited and looked real nice. Back in the bride's room, Linda and her bride's maids were all just divine. Out front the guests, mostly young people, were in excited anticipation over the evening's coming event, which was scheduled for seven o'clock. I was, as always, standing in the door through which the groom would enter. Don and the best man were right behind me.

At about one minute till seven, Linda's father came bursting into the auditorium. He entered shouting. Standing in the front of the room, he pointed his finger at the only black person there, a young man who worked with Don.

"The wedding's off. You hear me? It's all off. Ain't no daughter of mine getting married in no church where a nigger is. We ain't having no wedding here, not with that nigger present. It's off. Forget it."

The entire congregation was shocked totally beyond words. He caught them all by surprise. After all, who would have guessed such a thing? None of those people did.

Well, Dad then went to the bride's room, grabbed Linda by the arm, drug her out of the building, threw her in his car and drove off. There stood Don flabbergasted. There stood me wondering what to do next. It took about two minutes for the people to get their wits about them and regain their power of speech, Don included.

He walked out into the auditorium and spoke, "OK, everybody, I'm going to go to Linda's house to see what's going on. Just be calm. I'll be back soon."

They waited, but not quietly. The place was abuzz. Everyone had an opinion about what had happened. The young black fellow was especially hurt. He decided to go home. Several people apologized to him.

"Soon" turned into a half hour. Don finally got back with a brief message.

"Her dad says no. The wedding's off. Sorry."

The people left. I asked Don what he was going to do.

"I'm going back to Linda's house."

"Well, I'm going over to Neal's house. Let me know if I can do anything."

Neal was Don's former boss and his good friend. Neal and I had been close for a few years. During the time Don had been gone to Linda's we had decided to go over to his house with our wives. We did and, once there, we four sat around talking, mostly discussing the wedding that wasn't.

Meantime, Don did go to Linda's house, but he didn't go to the front door. He parked out of sight and walked to the window of her bedroom. There she sat in her wedding dress, crying. He tapped quietly on the glass and motioned to her to open it. As she did, he put his finger to his lip in a sign of quiet. They whispered. In a few minutes, they made a decision that she would change clothes, jump out the window and join him in an elopement.

In five minutes, she was ready and out and they were on the way. They came to Neal's house. We were all surprised.

"Hey, Buddy, will you do the wedding here, now?"

"Sure."

Neal had a piano in the living room. My wife, Becky, played the wedding march. Neal and his wife, Carol, stood up with the bride and groom. I did a ceremony. Everybody was happy. When it was over, Don and Linda proceeded to the planned honeymoon. The only thing missing was the reception.

The next Monday morning, Linda's dad showed up at Neal's shop.

"Hey," Neal said, "what was all that about the other night, breaking up the wedding and acting so stupid, insulting that man and making your daughter so unhappy?"

"It had nothing to do with that young man. I just needed something to use as an excuse. I wanted to see just how much they loved each other. I wanted them to prove they cared enough about each other to defy me. Now, I believe they really are in love and can overcome the problems of married life."

Good theory, rotten way to test it. It also proved nothing. The marriage only lasted a year.

So we come to the end of this book. As author, I truly hope you enjoyed it and received a blessing. I'm glad we could travel together in God's world for this brief time.

Remember this, knowledge is a gift from God to man. Gain all you can to His glory.

A Brief Message
To My Readers

As this book goes to press, I am making plans to write a sequel to it. It will mostly consist of my experiences in India, Mexico and Latvia. Look for it in the near future either at your bookseller or online. I am also making plans for some Bible study books based on the courses I have taught at college and church. The subject will be Biblical principles. Buy it for an exciting new look at some old truth. If you are a Christian teacher, either in church or college, you might want to consider it as a textbook. Look for all my future book online at iuniverse.com. Go there, click author search and type in Buddy Holbrook.

Thanks and God bless you.

About The Author

Buddy Holbrook, the son of a well-known Baptist pastor, has served God as a college and seminary teacher, preacher, pastor, conference speaker, missionary and evangelist. He has at one time or another served in every office a man can hold in an evangelical church. In years past, he has also had his own radio broadcasts, been a syndicated columnist and owned his own business. His travels have taken him throughout most of the USA, Mexico, South America, Europe and Asia. He is married to a lovely lady named Becky. They travel a lot. Their two grown children, Sallie and Jon also travel a lot. Must have got that from their Dad.

9 780595 153480